Daily Math Practice

GRADE 1

Manufacturer Evan-Moor Corporation
10 Harris Court, Suite C-3 Monterey, CA 93940, USA
www.evan-moor.com

EU Rep. Authorised Rep Compliance Ltd., Ground Floor,
71 Lower Baggot Street, Dublin, D02 P593, Ireland
www.arccompliance.com

Editorial Development: Marti Beeck
De Gibbs
Copy Editing: Cathy Harber
Art Direction: Cheryl Puckett
Cover Design: Yuki Meyer
Design/Production: Arynne Elfenbein
Susan Lovell
Jessica Onken

EVAN-MOOR Educational Publishers

EMC 750

Visit *teaching-standards.com* to view a correlation of this book.

Correlated to Current Standards

009

CPSIA: Sheridan Saline, Inc., Saline, MI, USA [7/2025]

The Value of *Daily Math Practice* in Your Classroom

Daily Math Practice helps make your students ready for their math lesson. Here's how!

In just 5 to 10 minutes each day, your students get these benefits:

- five short warm-up activities to complete independently
- practice in computation, a range of math skills, and a word problem
- review of both grade-level skills and previously learned skills

Short activities give students a wide variety of opportunities:

- working with graphics and models
- developing fluency with operations and processes
- understanding concepts and number relationships
- making sense of problems

You can extend *Daily Math Practice* into your lesson with these strategies:

- Encourage students to share and discuss their approaches to solving the problems, increasing each student's "solving toolkit."
- Invite students to identify patterns, explain concepts, and compare strategies with a partner or in a small group.
- Provide students with manipulatives and other mathematical tools to choose from, as well as scratch paper, to help them find solutions.
- Encourage students to check their own answers using a different method while asking themselves if their answers make sense.
- Check students' conceptual understanding by letting them discuss their reasoning and the procedures they used to solve problems.

What's in *Daily Math Practice*

Contents

36 Weekly Units

Days 1 through 4

Half-page activities offer scaffolded practice in grade-specific, standards-based skills. Each day's activity includes 5 math problems.

- 2 computation problems
- 1 word problem
- 2 questions or problems that apply a variety of math concepts

Day 5

A full-page activity provides more extensive practice of one or two target skills or reviews essential math concepts.

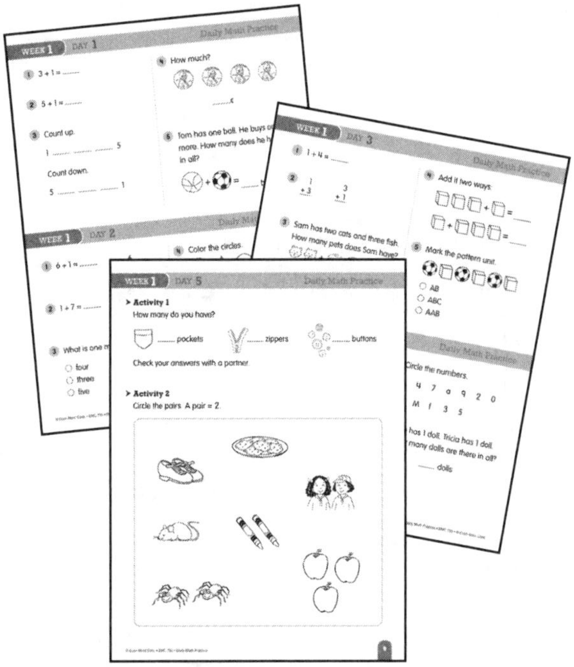

Additional Features

Scope and Sequence

The chart on pages 4 and 5 lists the skills practiced in the daily activities for each week.

Note that computation and operations are not listed as specific skills because they are a standard part of each day's activities.

Answer Key

Shows the answers for each day's activities in reduced-page format. The answer key begins on page 115.

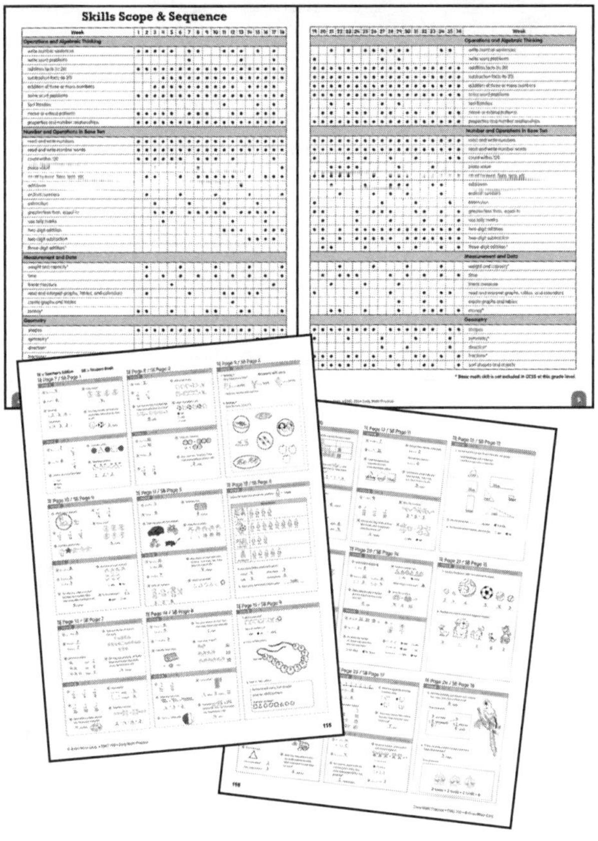

Skills Scope & Sequence

Week	1	2	3	4	5	6	7	8	9	10	11	12	13	14	15	16	17	18
Operations and Algebraic Thinking																		
write number sentences	●	●	●	●	●		●	●			●	●	●		●		●	
write word problems							●						●				●	
addition facts (to 20)	●	●	●	●	●	●	●	●	●	●	●	●	●	●	●	●	●	●
subtraction facts (to 20)				●	●	●	●	●	●	●	●	●	●	●	●	●	●	●
addition of three or more numbers			●	●	●	●	●	●	●	●	●	●		●	●	●	●	
solve word problems	●	●	●	●	●	●	●	●	●	●	●	●	●	●	●	●	●	●
fact families											●				●		●	
name or extend patterns	●	●	●	●	●		●	●	●			●	●		●	●	●	
properties and number relationships	●	●	●	●	●	●	●	●	●	●	●	●	●	●	●	●	●	●
Number and Operations in Base Ten																		
read and write numbers	●	●	●	●	●	●	●	●	●	●	●	●	●	●	●	●	●	●
read and write number words	●	●	●	●	●	●	●	●	●	●	●	●	●	●	●	●	●	●
count within 120	●	●	●	●	●	●		●	●	●		●					●	
place value			●					●										●
count by twos, fives, tens, etc.		●	●			●		●	●	●	●	●		●		●	●	●
odd/even													●					
ordinal numbers		●				●				●				●				●
estimation			●				●				●				●			
greater/less than, equal to			●	●	●		●	●	●	●	●		●	●	●	●	●	
use tally marks				●								●				●		
two-digit addition											●	●	●			●	●	●
two-digit subtraction														●	●	●	●	
three-digit addition																		
Measurement and Data																		
weight and capacity		●				●				●				●				●
time		●		●		●		●		●		●		●		●		●
linear measure					●												●	
read and interpret graphs, tables, and calendars		●					●				●	●		●	●			
create graphs and tables												●						
money	●	●			●				●	●			●	●				●
Geometry																		
shapes	●	●	●	●	●	●	●	●	●	●	●	●	●	●		●	●	●
symmetry															●			
direction																		
fractions			●				●				●	●			●	●		
sort shapes and objects	●	●		●		●	●	●		●		●	●			●	●	●

19	20	21	22	23	24	25	26	27	28	29	30	31	32	33	34	35	36	Week
																		Operations and Algebraic Thinking
		●		●		●	●	●	●	●	●				●	●		write number sentences
●								●		●								write word problems
●	●	●	●	●	●	●	●	●	●	●	●	●	●	●	●	●	●	addition facts (to 20)
●	●	●	●	●	●	●	●	●	●	●	●	●	●	●	●	●	●	subtraction facts (to 20)
●	●	●	●	●	●	●	●	●	●	●	●	●	●	●	●	●	●	addition of three or more numbers
●	●	●	●	●	●	●	●	●	●	●	●	●	●	●	●	●	●	solve word problems
		●		●				●		●								fact families
	●	●		●	●	●		●	●		●	●		●		●	●	name or extend patterns
●	●	●	●	●	●	●	●	●	●	●	●	●	●	●	●	●	●	properties and number relationships
																		Number and Operations in Base Ten
●	●	●	●	●	●	●	●	●	●	●	●	●	●	●	●	●	●	read and write numbers
●	●	●	●	●	●	●	●	●	●	●	●	●	●	●	●	●	●	read and write number words
●				●		●			●			●				●	●	count within 120
		●	●	●	●					●				●				place value
●	●	●	●	●			●		●	●	●		●	●	●	●	●	count by twos, fives, tens, etc.
		●				●			●	●	●			●	●			odd/even
			●				●		●		●				●			ordinal numbers
●								●				●				●		estimation
●	●				●		●	●	●			●	●		●		●	greater/less than, equal to
	●				●				●				●		●		●	use tally marks
●	●		●		●	●	●	●	●	●	●	●	●	●	●	●	●	two-digit addition
	●		●		●	●	●	●	●		●	●	●	●	●	●	●	two-digit subtraction
	●	●				●				●		●			●		●	three-digit addition
																		Measurement and Data
			●				●				●				●			weight and capacity
	●		●	●	●				●		●		●		●		●	time
		●				●				●								linear measure
●					●				●				●		●	●		read and interpret graphs, tables, and calendars
										●			●		●			create graphs and tables
		●	●			●				●			●	●	●		●	money
																		Geometry
●	●	●	●	●	●	●	●		●	●	●	●	●	●		●	●	shapes
●				●				●				●				●		symmetry
								●			●					●		direction
●	●	●		●	●		●		●			●	●		●		●	fractions
	●	●	●	●		●	●			●			●	●			●	sort shapes and objects

How to Use *Daily Math Practice*

1. Reproduce the activities for each five-day unit and cut apart the half-page lessons for days 1 through 4.
2. Consult the Scope & Sequence chart (pages 4 and 5) to identify any skills that are unfamiliar to your students. You may want to preview those skills as a whole-class activity.
3. Have students work independently, completing the daily lessons individually, with a partner, or in a small group.
4. Allow sufficient time for sharing solutions and discussing strategies. Modeling a variety of problem-solving techniques offers valuable learning benefits.

Teaching Tips:

- Provide students with any tools they need to complete each day's lesson.
- Establish a procedure for students to check their own work.
- Use a day's lesson as a quick, informal assessment.

Reproduce and distribute to students.

How to Solve Word Problems

1. **Read the word problem:** Make a picture of the problem in your mind.
   Ask yourself: What is the word problem about?
2. **Think about the problem some more:** Read the problem again.
   Think about the facts or details.
   Ask yourself: What do I need to find out?
3. **Draw a picture of the problem:** Draw a part for each number.
   Draw a part for the number you are trying to find.
   Ask yourself: What does each number mean?
4. **Solve the problem:** Decide what to do with the numbers.
   Ask yourself: What do I need to count, add, or subtract?
   Is there more than one step?
5. **Check your answer:** Write your answer in your picture.
   Ask yourself: Does my answer make sense?

1 $3 + 1 =$ _____

2 $5 + 1 =$ _____

3 Count up.

1 _____ _____ _____ 5

Count down.

5 _____ _____ _____ 1

4 How much?

_____¢

5 Tom has one ball. He buys one more. How many does he have in all?

 +  = _____ balls

1 $6 + 1 =$ _____

$$\begin{array}{r} 6 \\ +\ 1 \\ \hline \end{array}$$

2 $1 + 7 =$ _____

$$\begin{array}{r} 1 \\ +\ 7 \\ \hline \end{array}$$

3 What is one more than **two**?

- ○ four
- ○ three
- ○ five

4 Color the circles.

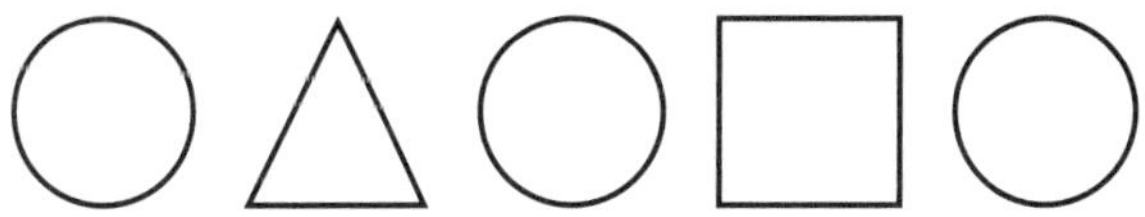

5 Write the numbers.

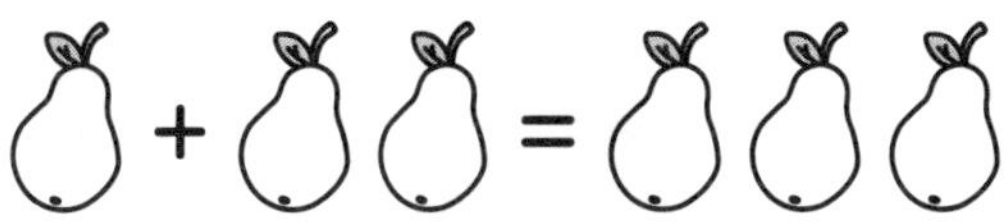

_____ + _____ = _____

1. 1 + 4 = ____

2.
```
  1       3
+ 3     + 1
---     ---
```

3. Sam has two cats and three fish. How many pets does Sam have?

____ pets

4. Add it two ways:

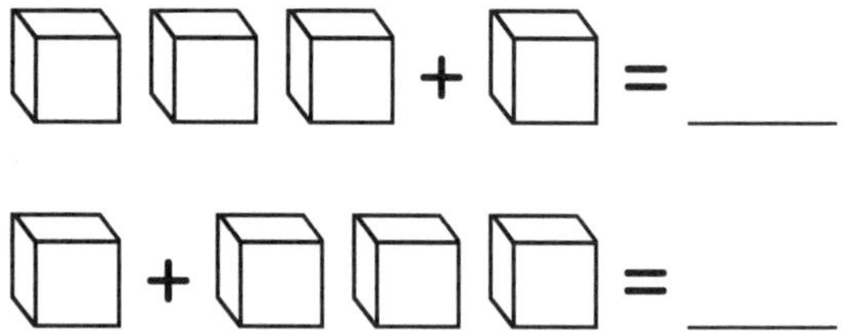

5. Mark the pattern unit.

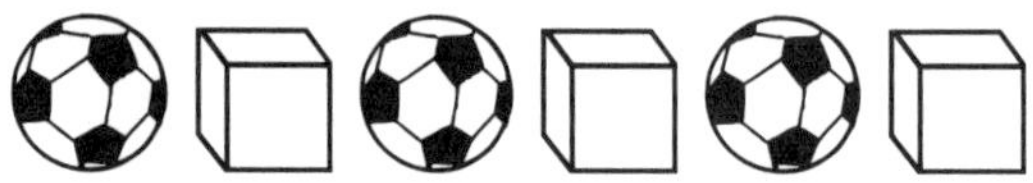

○ AB
○ ABC
○ AAB

1. 9 + 1 = ____

   1 + 9 = ____

2. 1 + 2 = ____

3.
```
  8       0
+ 0     + 8
---     ---
```

4. Circle the numbers.

4 7 a 9 2 0

M f 3 5

5. Ann has 1 doll. Tricia has 1 doll. How many dolls are there in all?

____ dolls

➤ Activity 1

How many do you have?

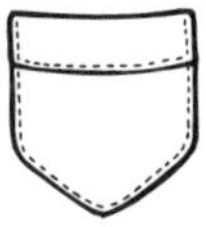 _____ pockets 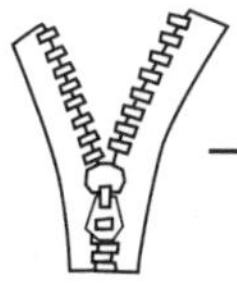 _____ zippers  _____ buttons

Check your answers with a partner.

➤ Activity 2

Circle the pairs. A pair = 2.

WEEK 2 DAY 1 Daily Math Practice

1 Which one is heavier?

2 $\begin{array}{r} 1 \\ +2 \\ \hline \end{array}$ $\quad$ $\begin{array}{r} 2 \\ +2 \\ \hline \end{array}$ $\quad$ $\begin{array}{r} 3 \\ +2 \\ \hline \end{array}$

3 Color the second one.

first

4 $\begin{array}{r} 4 \\ +2 \\ \hline \end{array}$ $\quad$ $\begin{array}{r} 2 \\ +4 \\ \hline \end{array}$

5 How much?

_____ cents

WEEK 2 DAY 2 Daily Math Practice

1 6 + 2 = _____

2 2 + 1 = _____

1 + 2 = _____

3 The bike rack is full. It has four big bikes and two little bikes. How many bikes are there in all?

_____ bikes

4 Are there enough mittens?

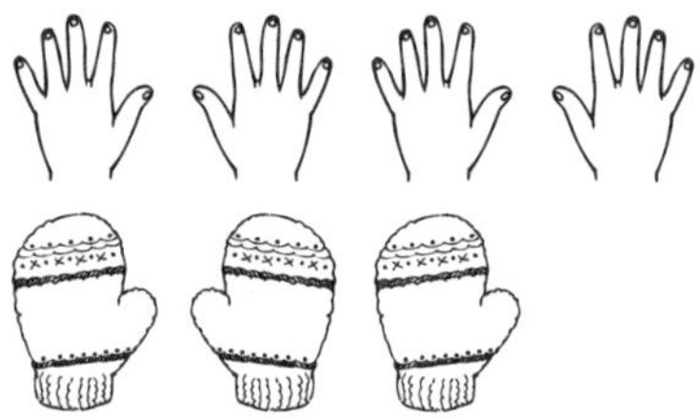

○ **yes** ○ **no**

5 Is this a triangle?

○ **yes** ○ **no**

1 2 + 7 = ____

2 3 + 2 = ____

3 Color the ones with four wheels.

4 Write the time.

____ o'clock

5 Write the numbers.

5 10 ____ ____ ____

1 8 + 2 = ____

2 + 8 = ____

2 5 + 2 = ____

3 Write the numbers.

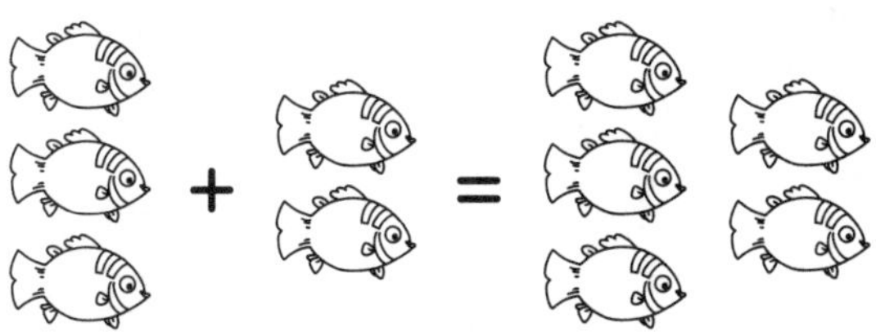

____ + ____ = ____

4 Mrs. Brown has two new pairs of shoes. How many new shoes does she have in all?

____ shoes

5 What comes next?

△ △ ○ △ △ ____

Look at the graph. Then answer the questions.  = **1 child**

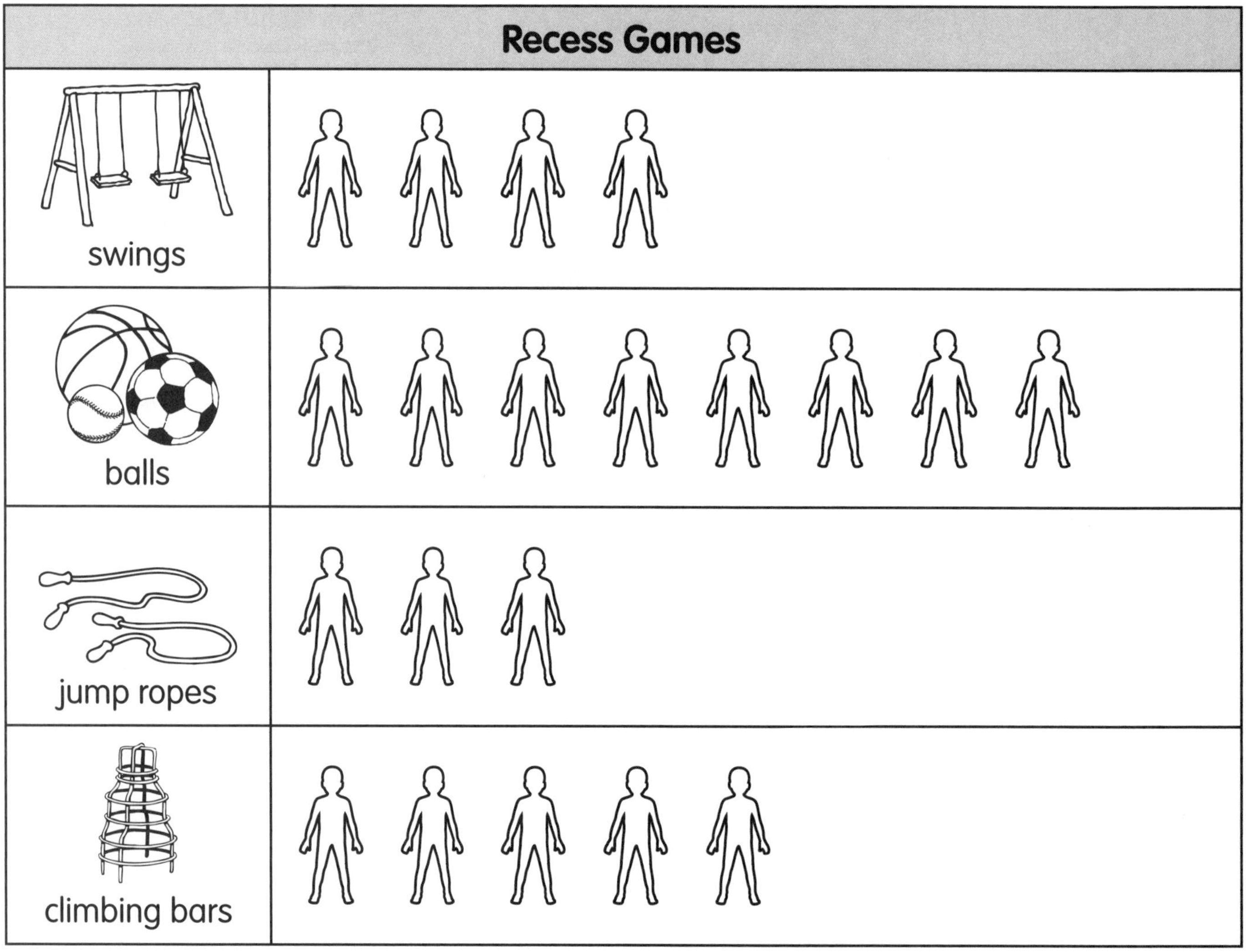

1. How many children played each game?

swings _____ jump ropes _____

balls _____ climbing bars _____

2. Which game did the most children play? ____________________

WEEK 3 DAY 1 Daily Math Practice

1. $3 + 5 =$ _____

2. $4 + 3 =$ _____

   $3 + 4 =$ _____

3. Write the number.

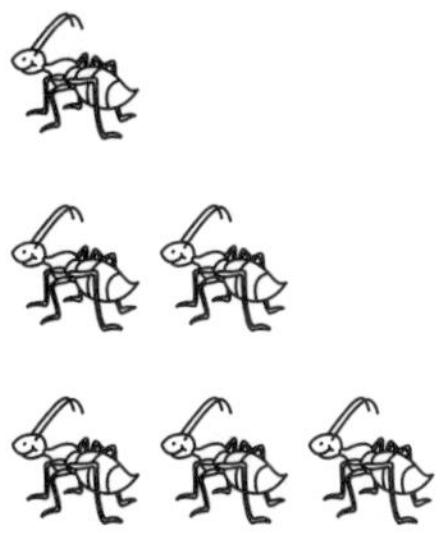

one _____

two _____

three _____

4. Write = in the box if they are the same.

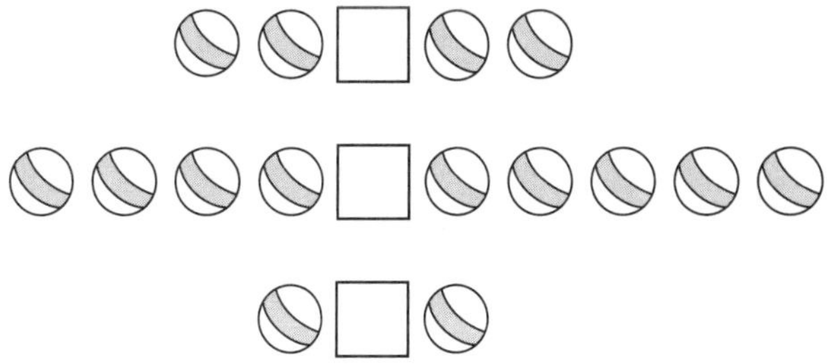

5. The dog had one bone. He found three more bones. How many bones did he have in all?

_____ bones

WEEK 3 DAY 2 Daily Math Practice

1.

$$\begin{array}{r} 2 \\ +\,2 \\ \hline \end{array} \qquad \begin{array}{r} 3 \\ +\,3 \\ \hline \end{array} \qquad \begin{array}{r} 4 \\ +\,4 \\ \hline \end{array}$$

2.

$$\begin{array}{r} 7 \\ +\,3 \\ \hline \end{array} \qquad \begin{array}{r} 6 \\ +\,4 \\ \hline \end{array} \qquad \begin{array}{r} 5 \\ +\,5 \\ \hline \end{array}$$

3. Mia had five cookies. She ate one. How many were left?

_____ cookies

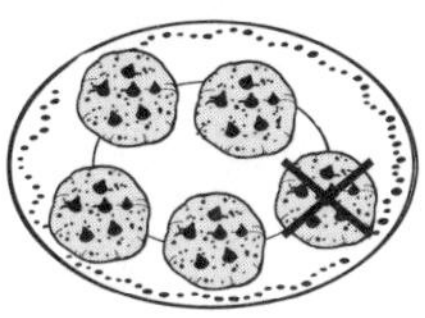

4. How many?

sides _____

corners _____

5. Write the numbers.

_____ + _____ = _____ + _____

1. $2 + 3 =$ ____

   $3 + 2 =$ ____

2. $1 + 1 + 1 =$ ____

3. About how many eggs?

2 12 100

4. Two birds were in the nest. One flew away. How many were left?

   ____ bird

5. How many fingers?

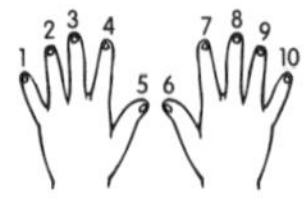

____

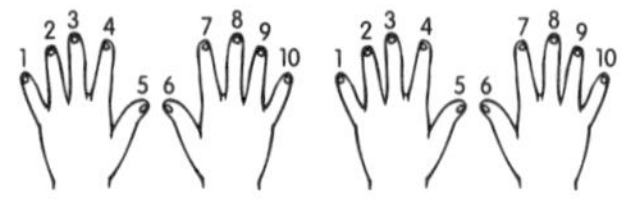

____

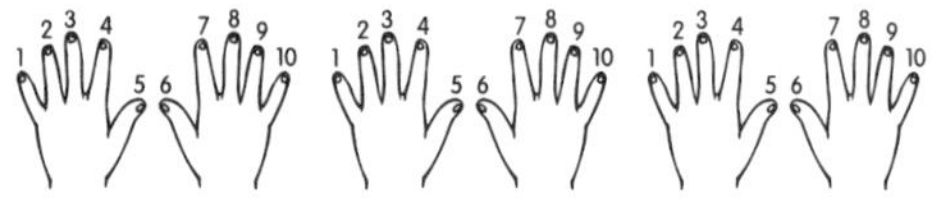

____

1.

3	8
+ 8	+ 3

2. Write the numbers.

 +  = 

____ + ____ = ____

3. Color $\frac{1}{2}$ of the ball.

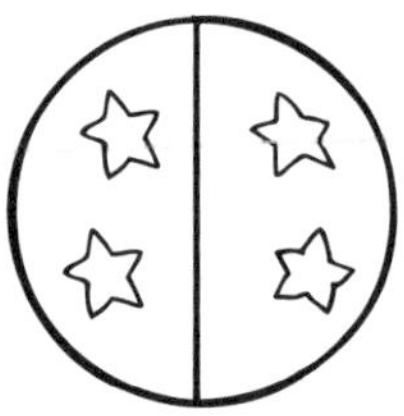

4. How many?

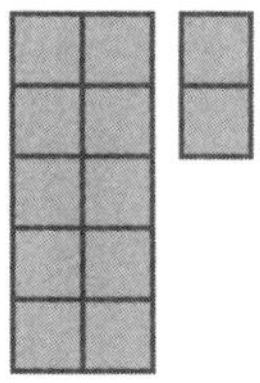

____ ten + ____ ones = ____

5. The train has a , a , and two  . How many cars does it have in all?

   ____ cars

1. What comes next?

Mark the pattern unit.

○ ABB ○ AB ○ ABCC

2. Color an AAB pattern.

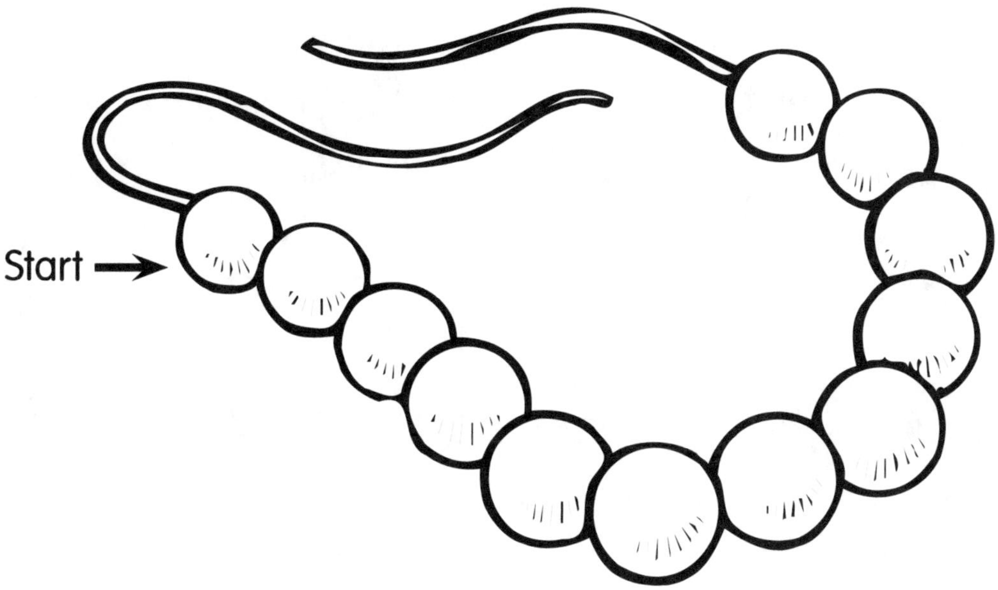

3. Draw an ABCC pattern.

1 4 + 5 = _____

2 2 + 4 = _____

3 What comes next?

 _____

Mark the pattern unit.

○ AB ○ ABC

4 Make one tally for each flower.

	|
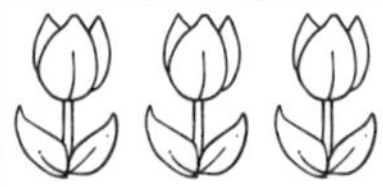	

5 Mary has two , one , and one . How many pets in all?

_____ + _____ + _____ = _____

1 4 + 4 = _____

5 + 5 = _____

2 4 + 6 = _____

3 Kai has one little , two little , three little . How many kittens does he have in all?

_____ kittens

4 Write the time.

_____ o'clock

5 Write the number.

six _____ eight _____

seven _____ nine _____

1 $4 + 3 =$ _____

2 $4 + 7 =$ _____

3 Color the square blue.
Color the circle red.
Color the triangle yellow.

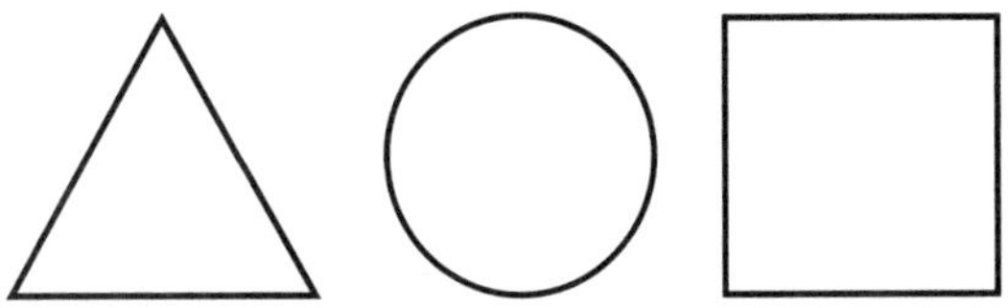

4 Bob put two cherries in the bowl.

$0 + 2 =$ _____

Bob ate two cherries.

$2 - 2 =$ _____

5 Luis has two green hats and three red hats. How many hats does he have in all?

_____ hats

1 $1 + 8 =$ _____

2 $\begin{array}{r} 8 \\ +4 \\ \hline \end{array}$ $\quad$ $\begin{array}{r} 7 \\ +4 \\ \hline \end{array}$ $\quad$ $\begin{array}{r} 6 \\ +4 \\ \hline \end{array}$

3 Rita has four big beads and two little beads. How many beads does she have in all?

_____ beads

4 Write the numbers.

_____ + _____ = _____

5 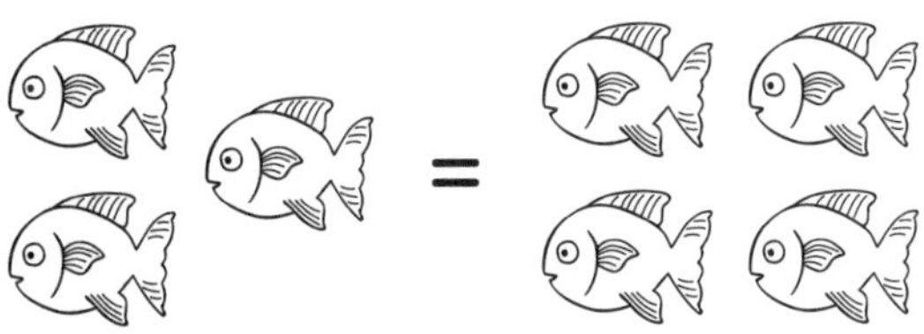

○ **yes** ○ **no**

1. You will color the shapes to sort them into two groups.

Color the shapes with 3 sides red.
Color the shapes with 4 sides blue.

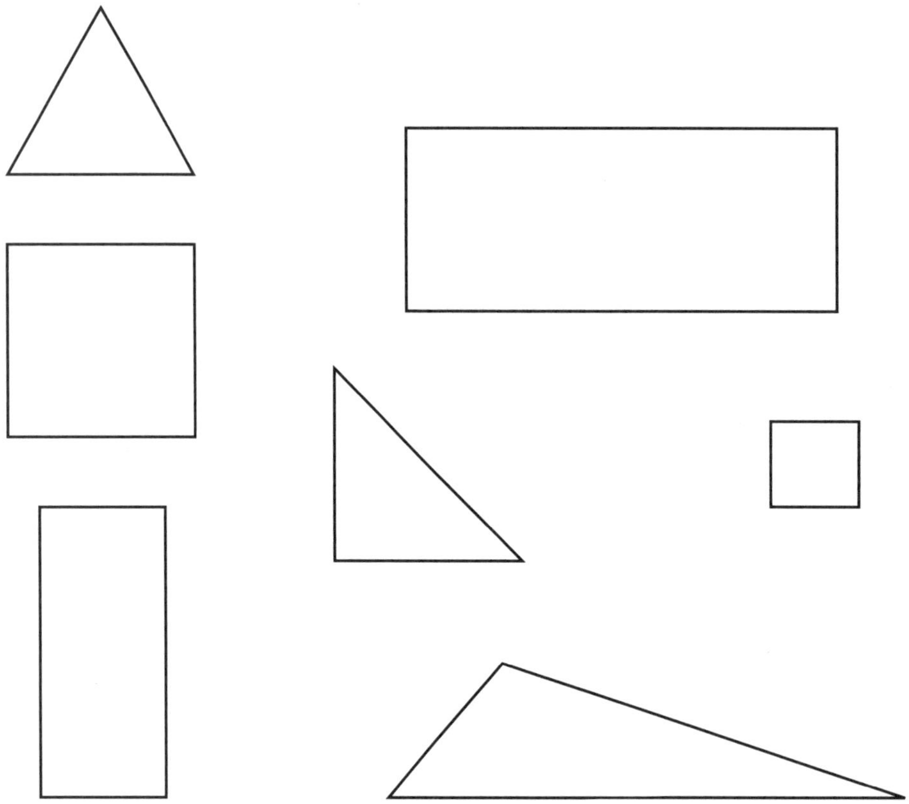

2. The red group has ____. ○ squares ○ triangles

3. The blue group has squares and triangles. ○ **yes** ○ **no**

1. 5 – 1 = _____

2. 7 – 1 = _____

3. What is 3 + 3? _____

   What is 4 + 4? _____

   What is 5 + 5? _____

4. How much?

_____ cents

5. How many stamps?

_____ stamps

1. 2 + 4 = _____

2. 10 – 1 = _____

   1 + _____ = 10

3. Count down.

   10 _____ _____ _____ _____ _____

   _____ _____ _____ _____ 0

4. 3 + 2 = 5 ○ **yes** ○ **no**

   2 + 3 = 5 ○ **yes** ○ **no**

   5 + 2 = 3 ○ **yes** ○ **no**

5. Sally ate two carrots, one apple, and four grapes. How many things did she eat?

   _____ things

1 

9 – 1 = ____

2 5 + 5 = ____ 4 + 4 = ____

3 + 3 = ____ 2 + 2 = ____

3 There were ten cats in the bed, and one rolled out. How many were left?

____ cats

4 Mark the pattern unit.

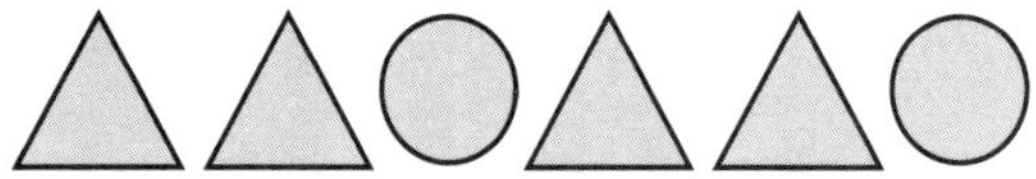

○ AB ○ AAB

What shape comes next? ______

5 Write the numbers.

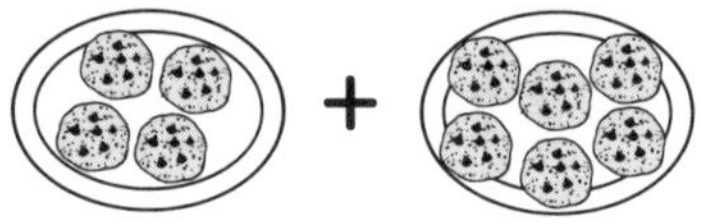 = ?

____ + ____ = ____

1 10 11 12 ____ ____ ____ 16

2 4 – 2 = ____

3 Mr. Black has five fish.
Mr. Brown has seven fish.
Who has more fish?

○ Mr. Black ○ Mr. Brown

4

$$\begin{array}{r} 6 \\ -\ 1 \\ \hline \square \end{array} \qquad \begin{array}{r} \square \\ +\ 1 \\ \hline 6 \end{array}$$

5 4 + 0 = 4 ○ **yes** ○ **no**

0 + 4 = 4 ○ **yes** ○ **no**

4 + 4 = 0 ○ **yes** ○ **no**

1. Number the balls in order from smallest to largest.

____ 1 ____ ____ ____ ____

2. Number the dogs in order from largest to smallest.

____ 1 ____ ____ ____

1. $5 - 2 =$ _____

2. $4 + 3 =$ _____

   $5 + 3 =$ _____

3. Mark has two pennies. His mom gives him three more pennies. How many pennies does he have in all?

   _____ pennies

4. What time is it?

- ○ 1 o'clock
- ○ 10 o'clock
- ○ 11 o'clock

5. Circle the third hat.

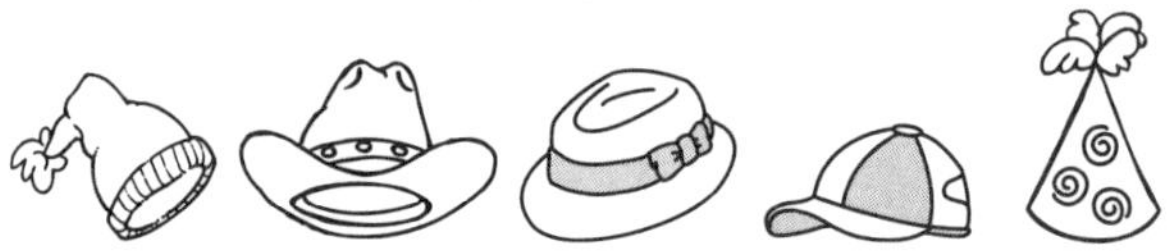

1. $8 - 2 =$ _____

2. $2 - 2 =$ _____

3. Draw a triangle.

   How many sides? _____

   How many corners? _____

4. Which is heavier? Circle it.

5. Sean has three letters to mail. He needs a stamp for each letter. How many stamps does he need?

   _____ stamps

1 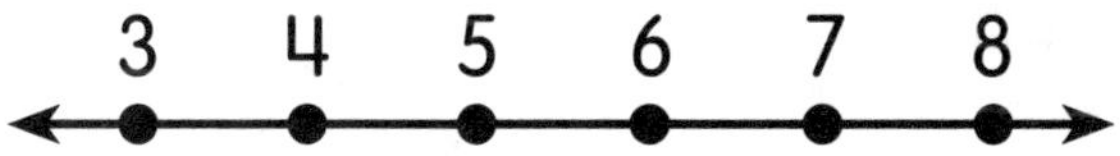

7 – 2 = _____

2 5 + 3 = _____

3 How many petals?

 5

 _____

 _____

 _____

4 Mark the square buttons that have two holes.

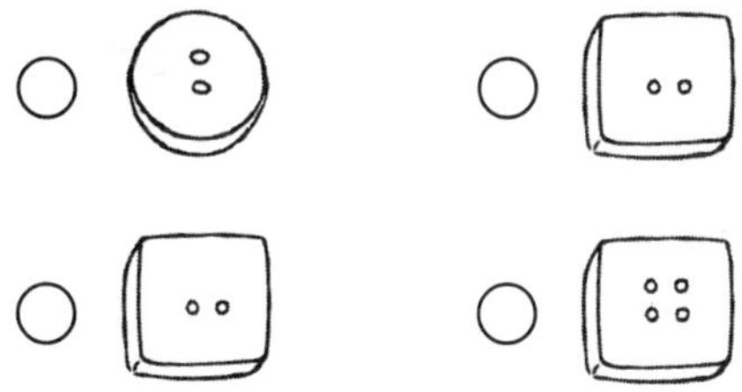

5 There were two red fish and five blue fish. How many fish were there in all?

_____ fish

1 6 – 2 = _____

6 – 4 = _____

2 4 + 5 = _____

3 Ron read six pages yesterday and four pages today. How many more pages did he read yesterday?

_____ more pages

4 Mark the number sentence that tells about the picture.

○ 3 + 2 = 6

○ 3 + 2 = 5

○ 3 – 2 = 5

5 3 + 1 – 1 = _____

1. Jack has 3 parrots, 2 parakeets, and 1 macaw. How many birds does he have in all?

_____ birds

Show your work.

2. If Jack can keep 2 birds in a cage, how many cages does he need?

_____ cages

Show your work.

WEEK 7 DAY 1 Daily Math Practice

1 

5 – 3 = _____

2 4 + 6 = _____

3 + 6 = _____

3 There were six eggs in the box. Two eggs broke. How many are left?

_____ eggs

4 Which is $\frac{1}{2}$?

○ 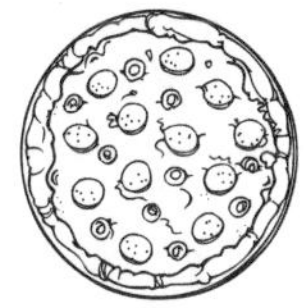 ○ 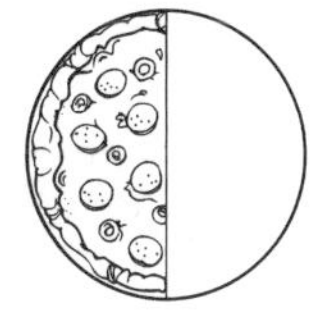

5 Write a story problem for

6 + 1 = ?

____

____

____

WEEK 7 DAY 2 Daily Math Practice

1 8 – 3 = _____

2 4 + 3 = _____

3 + 4 = _____

3 5 = 5 ○ **yes** ○ **no**

5 = 6 ○ **yes** ○ **no**

5 = 4 ○ **yes** ○ **no**

4 What comes next?

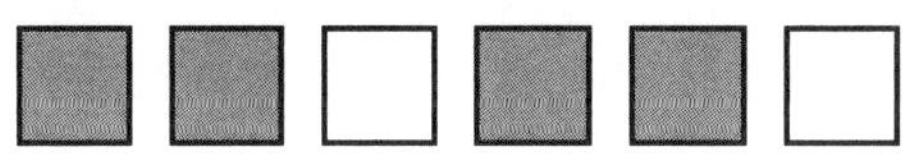 _____

5 There are two red beads, two blue beads, and two green beads. How many beads are there in all?

_____ beads

1 3 – 3 = _____

2 1 + 6 = _____

6 + 1 = _____

3 About how many potatoes?

○ 5 ○ 20 ○ 200

4 4 + 2 = 2 + 4 ○ yes ○ no

5 + 2 = 2 + 4 ○ yes ○ no

5 Write a number sentence to tell how many.

____

1 

9 – _____ = _____

2 6 + 3 = _____

3 Write the number.

ten _____

five _____

seven _____

4 Color the squares.

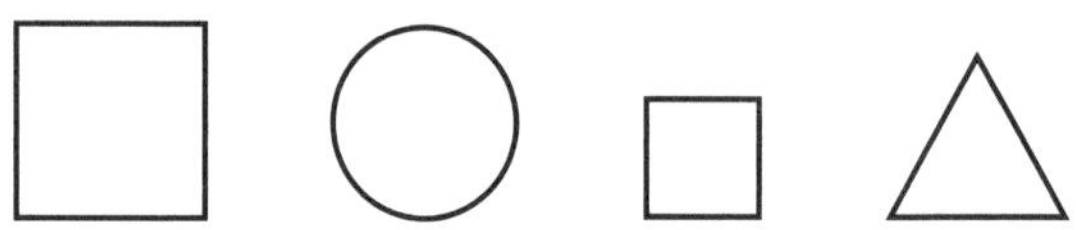

5 Tommy found three big feathers and three little feathers. How many feathers did he find in all?

_____ feathers

Mrs. Watson's class made a weather graph. Look at the graph to answer the questions.

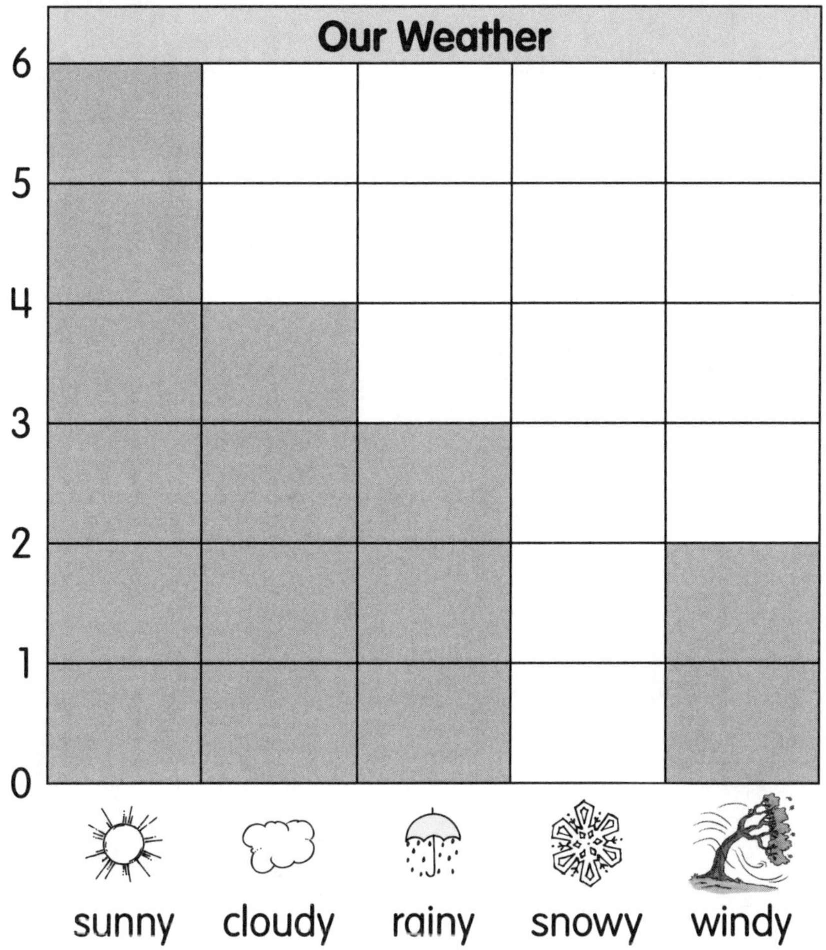

1. How many rainy days? ____

2. How many cloudy days? ____

3. Were there more rainy and cloudy days together than sunny days?

   ○ **yes** ○ **no**

4. Write something else you know from the graph.

____

WEEK 8 DAY 1 Daily Math Practice

1. 3 + 7 = _____

2.
```
  6        □
– 4      + 4
 ___     ___
  □        6
```

3. Each glass holds one cup of milk. How much milk is in six glasses?

   _____ cups

4.

ten	ones

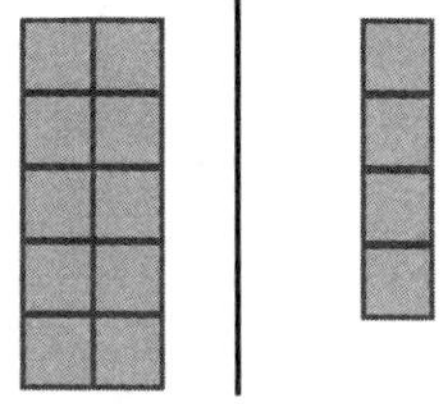

_____ ten + _____ ones = _____

5. What comes next?

   ○ △ △ ○ △ _____ _____

WEEK 8 DAY 2 Daily Math Practice

1. 8 – 4 = _____

2.
```
  6        3
+ 3      + 6
 ___     ___
```

3. There are five frogs on a log. If two frogs jump off, how many will be left?

   _____ frogs

4. What time is it?

○ 12:00
○ 9:00
○ 9:30

5. Write the numbers.

   two + three + four = nine

   _____ + _____ + _____ = _____

WEEK 8 DAY 3 Daily Math Practice

1. 10 + 10 = _____

2. $\begin{array}{r} 9 \\ -\ 4 \\ \hline \end{array}$ $\qquad$ $\begin{array}{r} 4 \\ +\ 9 \\ \hline \end{array}$

3. Five boys and five girls went on a hike. How many children hiked in all?

   _____ children

4. Count by twos.

_____ _____ _____ _____ _____

5. 4 < 4 ○ **yes** ○ **no**

   4 > 4 ○ **yes** ○ **no**

   4 = 4 ○ **yes** ○ **no**

WEEK 8 DAY 4 Daily Math Practice

1. 7 – 4 = _____

2. 10 – 5 = _____

3. There were 25 students in Mrs. White's class. Then 1 new student came. How many are in Mrs. White's class now?

   _____ students

4. Color the triangles.

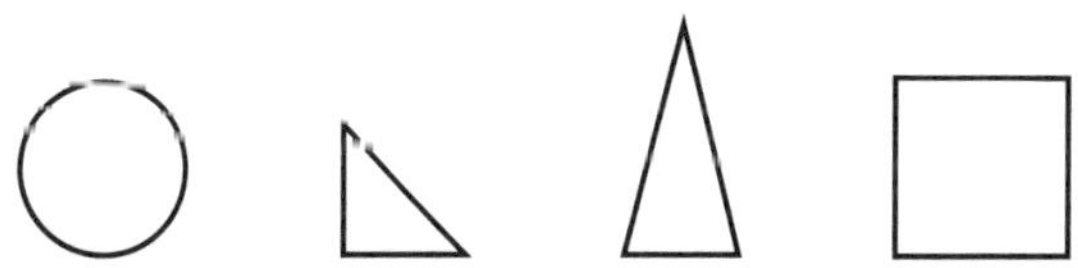

5. Write a number sentence.

_____ + _____ = _____

➤ Activity 1

Count from **1** to **50**.

	2			5					10
11					16				20
		23						29	
	32			35					
41						47			50

➤ Activity 2

Answer the questions.

How many ears do six elephants have? _____ ears

How many feet do four zebras have? _____ feet

How many tails do three monkeys have? _____ tails

WEEK 9 DAY 1 Daily Math Practice

1. 9 – 5 = _____

2. 4 + 6 = _____

   6 + 4 = _____

3. Wes has two bags of candy. Each bag has 6 pieces. How much candy does Wes have in all?

   _____ pieces

4. Are the teams equal?

○ yes ○ no

5. How much?

_____ cents

WEEK 9 DAY 2 Daily Math Practice

1. 8 – 5 = _____

2. $\begin{array}{r} 4 \\ +\,5 \\ \hline \square \end{array}$ $\begin{array}{r} \square \\ -\,4 \\ \hline 5 \end{array}$

3. There are five eggs in a nest. If one egg breaks, how many will be left?

   _____ eggs

4. Count back.

   20 19 18 _____ _____

   _____ _____ _____ _____

5. How many tens?

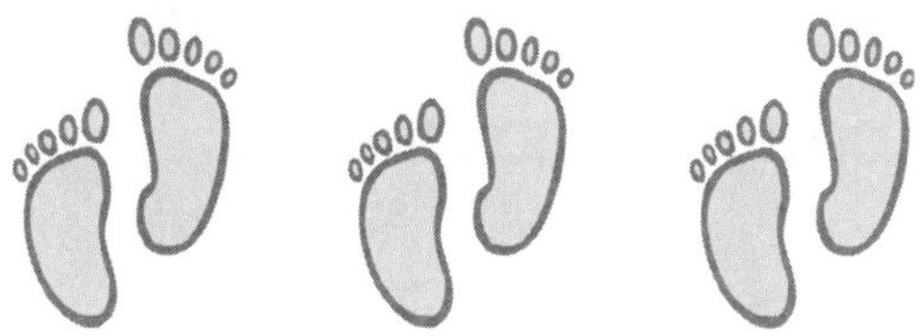

_____ tens

WEEK 9 DAY 3 Daily Math Practice

1. 3 + 3 + 2 = _____

2. 9 – 6 = _____

   10 – 6 = _____

3. Maria's coat has 4 buttons in the front and 2 on each sleeve. How many buttons does Maria's coat have in all?

   _____ buttons

4. 3 + 4 = 7 ○ yes ○ no

   4 – 7 = 3 ○ yes ○ no

   4 + 3 = 7 ○ yes ○ no

   7 – 3 = 4 ○ yes ○ no

5. A square has three equal sides.

   ○ yes ○ no

   Draw a square.

WEEK 9 DAY 4 Daily Math Practice

1. 10 – 4 = _____

2. 7 + 2 = _____

   _____ – 7 = 2

3. Josh has three beanbags, and Todd has four.

   Who has more? __________

   How many more? _____

4. Mark the pattern unit.

   ○ AB ○ AAB ○ ABB

5. What comes next?

   19 20 21 _____

   47 48 49 _____

Activity 1

Write your name in two different patterns.

Examples:

Pattern:	PEtePEtePEte	PeTePeTePeTe
Pattern Unit:	AABB	AB

Name the pattern unit. ________

Name the pattern unit. ________

Activity 2

Write the missing numbers.

10 20 30 ____ ____ 60 ____ ____ ____ ____ ____

5 10 15 ____ 25 ____ ____ ____ ____ ____ ____

2 4 6 ____ 10 12 ____ ____ ____ ____ ____ ____

1. $12 - 2 =$ ____

2.
$$\begin{array}{r} 5 \\ 3 \\ +\ 1 \\ \hline \end{array} \qquad \begin{array}{r} 5 \\ +\ 4 \\ \hline \end{array}$$

3. The apple tree had six apples. Bob picked two. How many apples were left?

   ____ apples

4. Color the fifth duck.

5. $4 + 2 = 6$ ○ **yes** ○ **no**

   $3 + 3 = 6$ ○ **yes** ○ **no**

   $6 + 0 = 6$ ○ **yes** ○ **no**

   $5 + 2 = 6$ ○ **yes** ○ **no**

1. $10 - 7 =$ ____

   $11 - 7 =$ ____

2. $8 + 3 =$ ____

3. Jenny picked up two pennies. She put them with her other six pennies. How many pennies does Jenny have now?

   ____ pennies

4. Circle the hats that have stripes and bills.

5. Write the time.

____ o'clock

1 $5 + 2 + 4 =$ _____

2 What number is one less?

_____ 13

_____ 26

3 Sue had a double scoop of ice cream. Tom had a triple scoop. Who had the smallest amount?

○ Sue ○ Tom

4 How many?

 = _____ 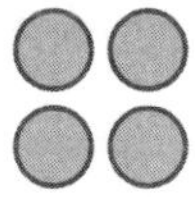 = _____

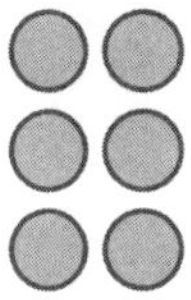 = _____ 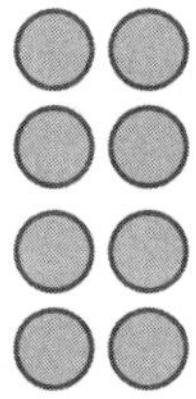 = _____

5 Which weighs more?

○  ○ 

1 $9 - 8 =$ _____

$12 - 11 =$ _____

2 $9 + 7 =$ _____

3 Tommy had 10 cents. He bought a pencil for 5 cents. How much does he have left?

_____ cents

4 Color the squares.

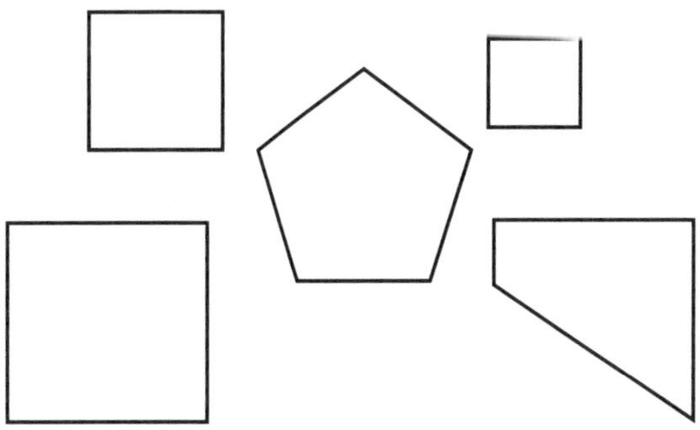

5 Four cherries and five grapes equal _____ pieces of fruit.

Activity 1

Use the number line to solve the problem.

10 − 5 + 6 − 1 + 4 − 2 = _____

Show your work here.

Activity 2

Count from **51** to **110**.

51	52	53							60
					66		68		
71			74						80
				85					
								99	
101	102	103				107			110

WEEK 11 DAY 1 Daily Math Practice

1. 5 + 5 = _____

   5 + 4 = _____

2. 12 – 2 = _____

3. Juan's family ate four tortillas for lunch and four tortillas for dinner. How many did they eat in all?

   _____ tortillas

4. Write the number.

   eight _____

   four _____

   twelve _____

   zero _____

5. 2 + 2 + 2 + 2 = _____

   10 + 10 + 10 + 10 = _____

WEEK 11 DAY 2 Daily Math Practice

1. 8 + 3 = _____

   _____ – 8 = 3

2. 3 + 2 + 3 = _____

3. I saw six sea stars, three snails, and a sunfish at the beach. How many animals did I see?

   _____ animals

4. Color $\frac{1}{2}$. Color 1 whole.

5. 5 + 4 = 4 + 5

   ○ **yes** ○ **no**

   6 + 4 = 4 + 5

   ○ **yes** ○ **no**

1. 10 + 9 = _____

   _____ − 10 = 9

2. 2 + 6 = _____

3. $10 = 5 + 4$ ○ **yes** ○ **no**

   $10 < 5 + 4$ ○ **yes** ○ **no**

   $10 > 5 + 4$ ○ **yes** ○ **no**

4. Draw three circles.

   Color one blue. Color two red.

   Write a number sentence to tell about the circles.

   _____ + _____ = _____

5. 5 boys + 5 girls + 1 dog = _____

1. 

   45 + 3 = _____

2. 

   17 − 5 = _____

3. Three girls each have three bears. How many bears do they have in all?

   _____ bears

4. About how many crayons?

   ○ almost 6

   ○ almost 20

   ○ almost 160

5. Write four number sentences using **4**, **2**, and **6**.

   _____ + _____ = _____

   _____ + _____ = _____

   _____ − _____ = _____

   _____ − _____ = _____

For nine months, the students in Mrs. Timm's class put a on a graph every time one of them lost a tooth. Look at the graph to answer the questions.

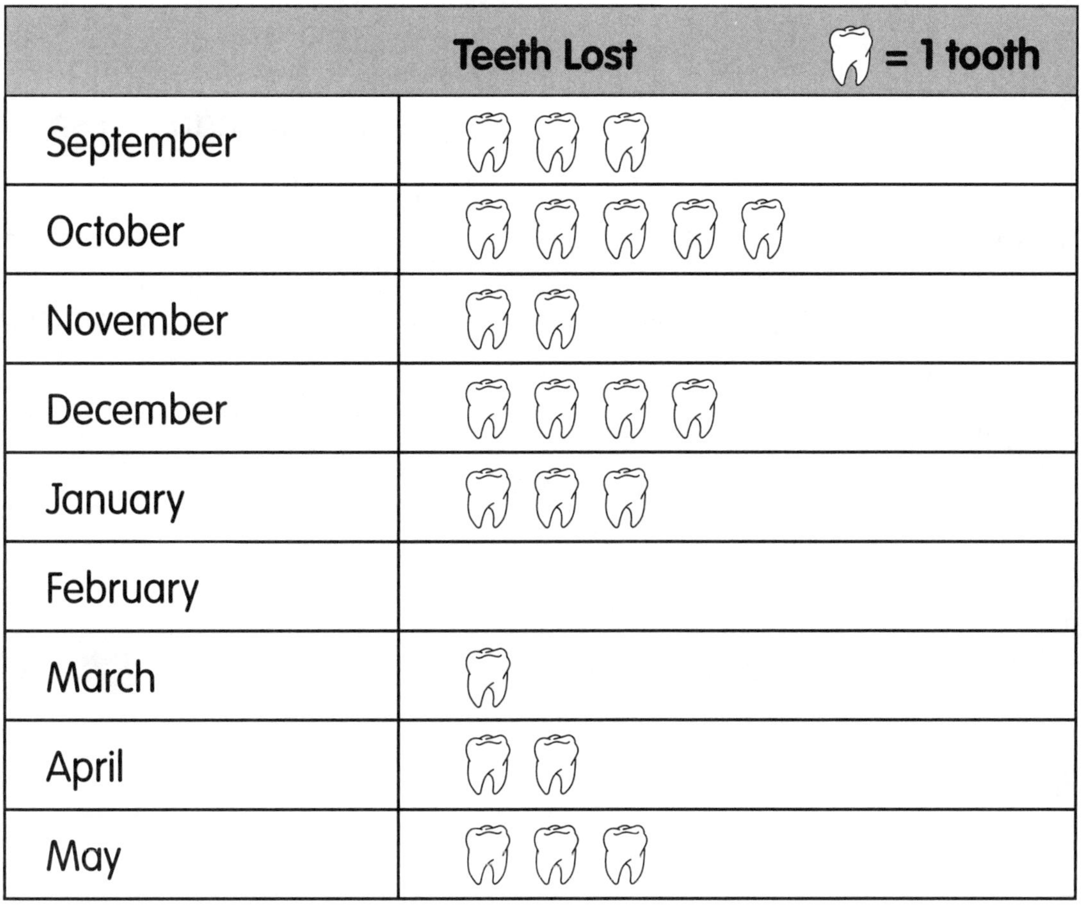

1. How many teeth have been lost in all? _____ teeth

2. In which month were the most teeth lost?

   ○ February ○ October ○ May

3. In which month were the fewest teeth lost?

   ○ March ○ September ○ February

1.
$$\begin{array}{r} 4 \\ +\ 3 \\ \hline \end{array} \qquad \begin{array}{r} 14 \\ +\ 3 \\ \hline \end{array}$$

2.
$$\begin{array}{r} 7 \\ -\ 4 \\ \hline \end{array} \qquad \begin{array}{r} 7 \\ -\ 3 \\ \hline \end{array}$$

3. Mr. Smith sold two bags of oranges. If each bag has eight oranges, how many oranges did he sell in all?

_____ oranges

4. Write the time.

_____ o'clock

5. Draw tally marks to show how many.

1. 6 + 6 = _____

6 + 6 + 6 = _____

2. 30 + 20 = _____

3. There are two raisins on each cookie. How many raisins are there on three cookies?

_____ raisins

4. Continue the pattern.

2 2 1 2 2 1 _____ _____ _____

_____ _____ _____

5. Count the eyes.

_____ _____ _____ _____

1 How many?

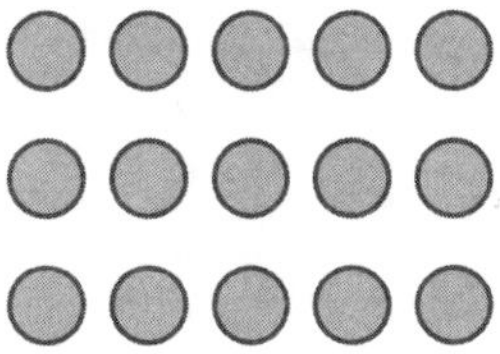 = _____

2 54 + 1 = _____

3 There are two peanuts in each shell. How many peanuts are in six shells?

_____ peanuts

4 Draw an **X** on the spheres.

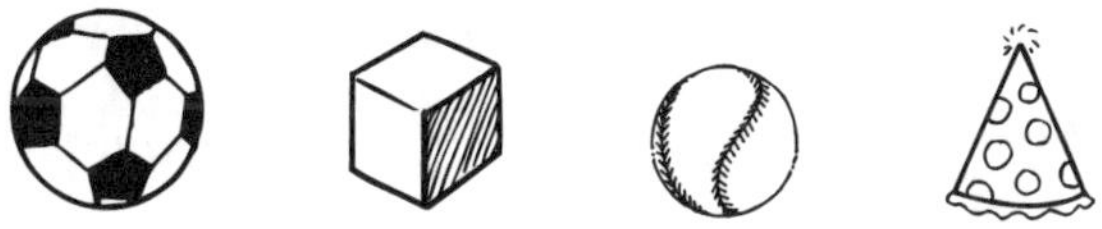

5 Add two.

5 + 2 = _____

Then subtract two.

_____ − 2 = _____

1 4 + 3 + 2 + 1 = _____

2 13 − 7 = _____

7 + _____ = 13

3 Jose read two books every day. How many books did he read in five days?

_____ books

4 Write the number.

thirty-six _____

twenty-seven _____

5 Draw an **X** on $\frac{1}{4}$.

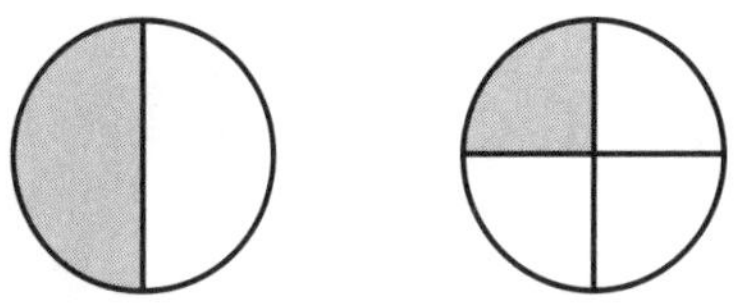

Sienna went to the store to buy snacks. She bought four muffins, six oranges, and five carrots.
Draw the snacks on the chart.

muffins 	oranges 	carrots 

Use the chart to answer the questions.

1. How many snacks did Sienna buy in all?

_____ + _____ + _____ = _____ snacks

2. Sienna ate one muffin. How many snacks does she have now?

_____ − _____ = _____ snacks left

WEEK 13 DAY 1 Daily Math Practice

1 How many?

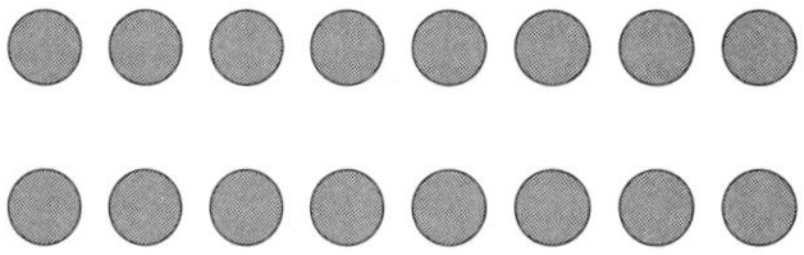

= _____

2 20 – 10 = _____

3 Carl rode his bike two blocks to the park and two blocks home. How far did he ride?

_____ blocks

4 Which pattern is shown below?

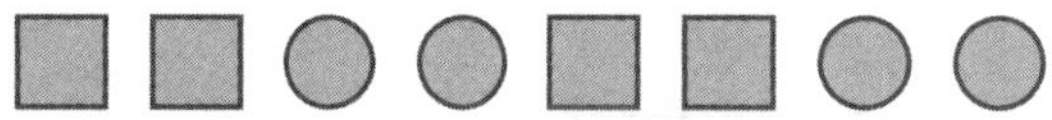

○ ABA ○ AABB ○ ABBA

5 How much?

_____ cents

WEEK 13 DAY 2 Daily Math Practice

1 0 + 15 = 7 + 8

○ **yes** ○ **no**

2 2 + 9 = _____

3

$$\begin{array}{r} 3 \\ +\,4 \\ \hline \square \end{array} \qquad \begin{array}{r} \square \\ -\,3 \\ \hline 4 \end{array}$$

4 Draw an **X** on the circles.

5 Brett and Bonnie ate pizza for lunch. They each had four pieces. How many pieces did they eat in all?

_____ pieces

1. $6 + 4 =$ ____

   $7 + 3 =$ ____

2. $14 - 13 =$ ____

3. $1 + 15 = 16$ ○ **yes** ○ **no**

   $15 + 1 = 16$ ○ **yes** ○ **no**

   $16 + 1 = 15$ ○ **yes** ○ **no**

4. Write a story problem about birds for **5 – 2 = 3**.

   ____

   ____

   ____

   ____

5. How much?

   = ____¢

1. $6 + 4 < 7 + 7$

   ○ **yes** ○ **no**

2. $14 - 2 =$ ____

3. Seline put three cookies and two brownies in a box for her grandma. How many treats will her grandma have altogether?

   ____ treats

4. Circle **odd** or **even**.

    **odd** **even**

    **odd** **even**

   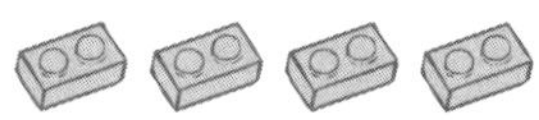 **odd** **even**

5. Circle the ways to make **7**.

$5 + 2$	$4 + 4$	$6 + 1$
$9 - 2$	$3 + 5$	$7 + 0$

1. Mark has to buy two new tires for his bike. If each tire costs $10.00, how much money does Mark need?

$________

2. Mark has $15.00 in his bank, and he got $5.00 for doing jobs. Can he buy the tires?

○ **yes** ○ **no**

Explain:

____

____

____

____

1 $3 + 9 =$ ____

$9 + 3 =$ ____

2 $15 + 1 =$ ____

____ $- 1 = 15$

3 Sammy found two nickels in his pocket. How much did he find?

____¢

4 Draw an **X** on the seventh bird.

5 5 10 15 ____ ____ ____

____ ____ ____ ____

____ ____ ____ ____

1 $2 + 9 =$ ____

$2 + 10 =$ ____

$2 + 11 =$ ____

2 $\begin{array}{r} 11 \\ -\ 5 \\ \hline \end{array}$ $\qquad$ $\begin{array}{r} 11 \\ -\ 6 \\ \hline \end{array}$

3 Which is heavier?

10 pounds 100 pounds

4 Write the time.

____ o'clock

5 There were six flowers in the vase. Two of the flowers were roses. How many flowers were **not** roses?

____ flowers

WEEK 14 DAY 3 Daily Math Practice

1. 5 + 6 = _____

   6 + 5 = _____

2. 16 – 8 = _____

   8 + _____ = 16

3. Trina saw three pigs, two cows, and four chickens on the farm. How many animals did she see in all?

   _____ animals

4. Draw a rectangle.

   Write how many.

   _____ sides _____ corners

5. 12 = 4 + 8 ○ **yes** ○ **no**

   8 = 12 + 4 ○ **yes** ○ **no**

   12 = 8 + 4 ○ **yes** ○ **no**

WEEK 14 DAY 4 Daily Math Practice

1. 7 – 5 = _____

   8 – 5 = _____

2. 4 + 8 = _____

3. Five pairs of ants marched up the hill. How many ants were there in all?

   _____ ants

4. Circle the ways to make **nine**.

   3 + 6 4 + 5 2 + 7

   1 + 7 0 + 9 4 + 4

5. How much?

   _____ cents

1. How many toes?

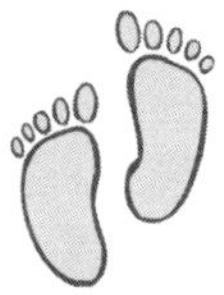

_____ toes

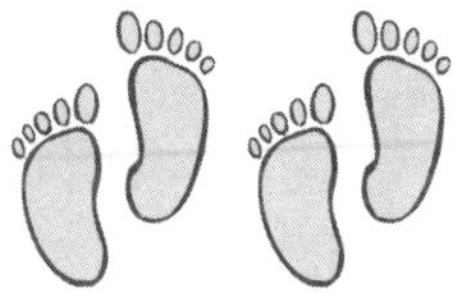

_____ toes

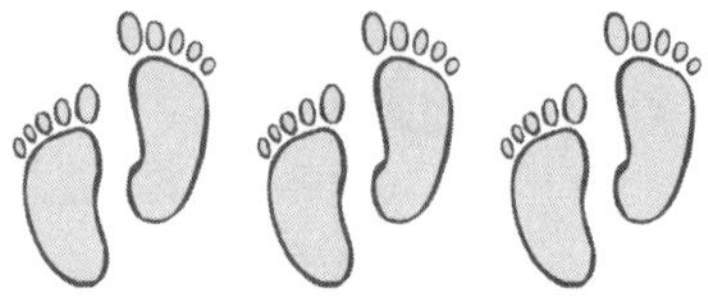

_____ toes

How many toes do 5 babies have? _____ toes

2. How many ears?

_____ ears

_____ ears

_____ ears

How many ears do 6 rabbits have? _____ ears

WEEK 15 DAY 1 Daily Math Practice

1 5 + 7 = 11 + 0

○ **yes** ○ **no**

2 10 – 3 = _____

20 – 3 = _____

3 There were two goldfish and four red fish in the bowl. How many fish were there in all?

_____ fish

4 Are the two sides the same?

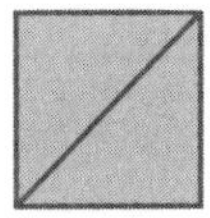

○ **yes** ○ **no**

○ **yes** ○ **no**

5 Finish the pattern.

WEEK 15 DAY 2 Daily Math Practice

1 5 + 8 = _____

8 + 5 = _____

2 4 – 4 = _____

25 – 25 = _____

3 The bag had ten cookies in it. If Eli ate two and Molly ate one, how many cookies were left?

_____ cookies

4 Mark the pizza divided in half.

○  ○ 

5 Write the number.

eleven _____

thirteen _____

fourteen _____

WEEK 15 DAY 3 — Daily Math Practice

1. 7 + 5 = ____

   ____ − 7 = 5

2. 4 + 2 + 1 = ____

3. $9 < 3$ ○ yes ○ no

   $19 > 13$ ○ yes ○ no

4. About how many paper clips?.

○ 5
○ 15
○ 50

5. Bingo hid four bones in the garden and two bones in the park. How many bones did he hide in all?

   ____ bones

WEEK 15 DAY 4 — Daily Math Practice

1.

4	5	6
+ 9	+ 8	+ 7

2. 18 − 1 = 17 + 0

   ○ yes ○ no

3. Four trucks and six cars were stopped at a light. How many vehicles were stopped in all?

   ____ vehicles

4. Write four number sentences using **3**, **5**, and **8**.

   ____ + ____ = ____

   ____ + ____ = ____

   ____ − ____ = ____

   ____ − ____ = ____

5. Are both sides the same?

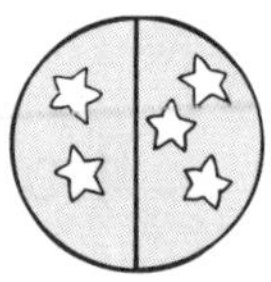

   ○ yes ○ no

Activity 1

 = 1 birthday

March						
Sun.	Mon.	Tues.	Wed.	Thurs.	Fri.	Sat.
			1	2	3	 4
5	6	 7	8	9	10	11
12	13	 14	15	16	 17	18
19	20	21	22	23	24	25
26	27	 28	29	30	31	

1. How many birthdays are there in March? _____ birthdays

2. What day of the week has the most birthdays?

   ○ Sunday ○ Tuesday ○ Friday

3. There is only one birthday on the weekend. ○ **yes** ○ **no**

Activity 2

Use this number line to mark **yes** or **no** for each number sentence.

1. $10 > 11$ ○ **yes** ○ **no**

2. $14 = 13 + 1$ ○ **yes** ○ **no**

3. $12 < 9$ ○ **yes** ○ **no**

4. $7 > 3$ ○ **yes** ○ **no**

WEEK 16 DAY 1 Daily Math Practice

1 6 + 8 = _____

8 + 6 = _____

2 15 − 7 = _____

_____ + 7 = 15

3 What comes next?

2 4 6 8 10 12 14 _____

4 Which shows $\frac{1}{4}$?

○ 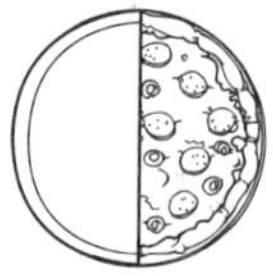   ○ 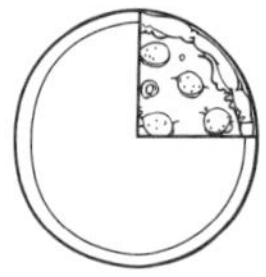

5 Keli is 11. Her sister is 6. How many years older than her sister is Keli?

_____ years older

WEEK 16 DAY 2 Daily Math Practice

1 7 + 7 = _____

7 − 7 = _____

2 10 + 10 + 10 = _____

3 Tony swam four laps of freestyle and six laps of backstroke. How many laps did he swim in all?

_____ laps

4 Continue the pattern.

□ △ ○ □ △ ○

_____ _____ _____

5 How many?

○ 11   ○ 12   ○ 21

WEEK 16 DAY 3 Daily Math Practice

1. 7 – 6 = 1 + 0

   ○ **yes** ○ **no**

2. 9 + 3 = _____

   9 + 4 = _____

3. I have seven sharp pencils and two broken pencils. How many pencils do I have in all?

   _____ pencils

4. If 53 + 4 = 57, then 57 – 4 = _____.

5. Write the number.

   four _____

   twenty-one _____

   thirty _____

   thirty-two _____

WEEK 16 DAY 4 Daily Math Practice

1. 6 + 10 = _____

   6 + 9 = _____

2. 10 – 2 = 7 – 0

   ○ **yes** ○ **no**

3. Jamal hit three balls. Ann hit four balls. Terri didn't get a hit. How many hits were there in all?

   _____ hits

4. What time is it?

   _____ o'clock

5. Color the bigger square.

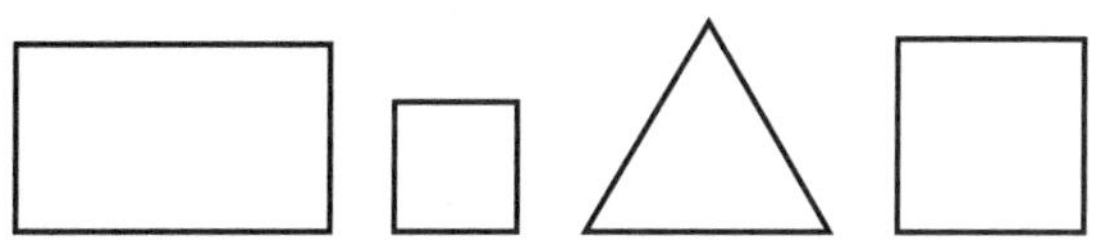

On Monday, four girls checked out 3 books each.
On Tuesday, two of the girls returned their books.

1. How many books are still checked out? _____ books

Show your work here.

2. Each girl reads 3 books every day. How many books will each girl read in 3 days?

_____ books

WEEK 17 DAY 1 Daily Math Practice

1. 7 + 8 = ____ ____ − 7 = 8

2. 9 + 2 = 11 + 0

   ○ **yes** ○ **no**

3. Two polar bears were walking across the ice. Six more polar bears joined them. How many were there in all?

   ____ polar bears

4. 35 34 33 ____ ____ ____ ____ ____ ____

5. Write four number sentences using **6**, **5**, and **11**.

   ____ + ____ = ____

   ____ + ____ = ____

   ____ − ____ = ____

   ____ − ____ = ____

WEEK 17 DAY 2 Daily Math Practice

1. 15 − 7 = ____ 15 − 8 = ____

2. 9 + 5 = ____

   7 + 7 = ____

3. Each drummer needs two drumsticks. How many drumsticks do five drummers need?

   ____ drumsticks

4. 3 + 3 + 3 = ____

   4 + 4 + 4 = ____

5. Write an addition story to tell about the fish.

____

____

____

1. 9 + 7 = _____

2. 9 – 2 = _____

   2 + _____ = 9

3. Juanita had three cupcakes. She gave one to Felix and two to the twins. How many cupcakes did she have left?

   _____ cupcakes

4. 10 20 30 _____ _____ _____

   _____ _____ _____ _____

5. How many sides?

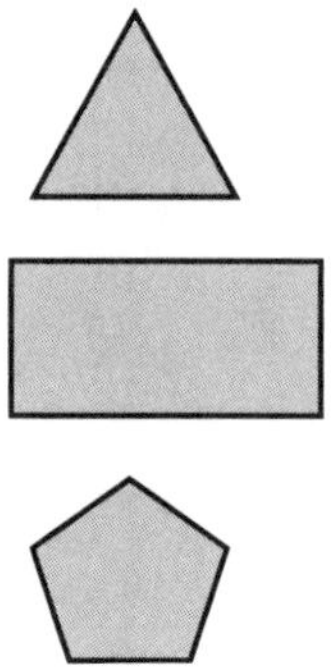

_____

_____

_____

1. 8 + 5 = _____

2. 20 – 10 = _____

3. The hungry caterpillar ate three leaves, two strawberries, and five grapes. How many things did it eat in all?

   _____ things

4. Write the rule for each group.

Group 1

____

____

____

Group 2

____

____

____

5. If 34 + 7 = 41, then

   41 – _____ = 34.

1. Measure the **longest** side of a book with your pencil.

   My book is ____ pencils long.

2. Look at the picture to answer the questions.

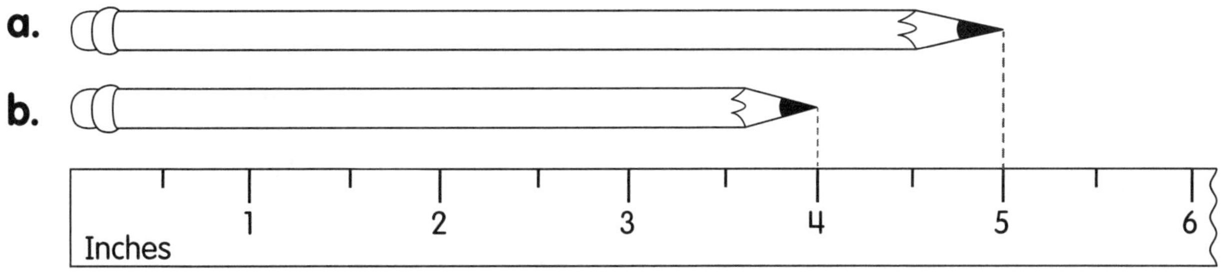

   Color the longer pencil yellow.

   Color the shorter pencil red.

   How long is each pencil? **a.** ____ inches **b.** ____ inches

   How much longer is the yellow pencil than the red pencil?

   ____ inch longer

3. Add or subtract.

2 inches	5 inches	3 inches
+ 3 inches	− 1 inch	+ 3 inches
☐ inches	☐ inches	☐ inches

1 $7 + 9 =$ _____

$7 + 11 =$ _____

2 $15 - 9 =$ _____

$15 - 6 =$ _____

3 Which is heavier? Circle it.

2 grams	51 pounds
20 grams	15 pounds

4 Draw an **X** on the eighth bead.

first →

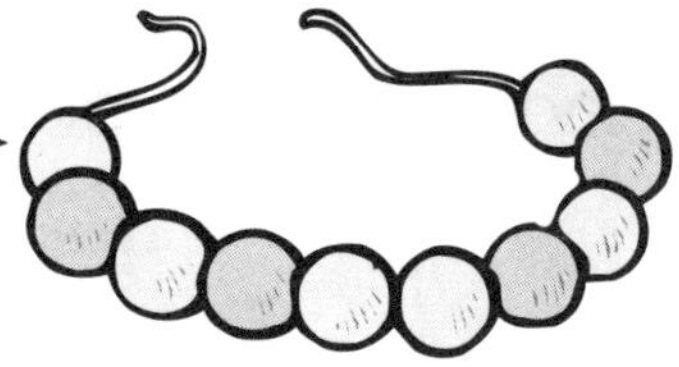

5 Lilly drew five hearts. She colored two of them red. She colored the rest pink. How many hearts are pink?

_____ pink hearts

1

$$\begin{array}{r} 10 \\ +\ 0 \\ \hline \end{array} \qquad \begin{array}{r} 10 \\ +\ 5 \\ \hline \end{array} \qquad \begin{array}{r} 10 \\ +10 \\ \hline \end{array}$$

2 If $17 - 5 = 12$, then $12 + 5 =$ _____.

3 Circle the one that does **not** belong.

4 What time is it?

_____ o'clock

5 Mike invited seven friends to his party. Two cannot come. How many friends will be there?

_____ friends

WEEK 18 DAY 3 Daily Math Practice

1. 9 + 8 = ____

   ____ – 9 = 8

2. 5 + 10 = ____

   ____ – 5 = 10

3. Count by 5s.

   50 55 ____ ____ ____

   ____ ____

4. ____ tens + ____ ones = 76

   ____ tens + ____ ones = 50

5. David bought two apples for $1.00. How much would four apples cost?

   $________

WEEK 18 DAY 4 Daily Math Practice

1. 5 + 10 = ____

   5 + 9 = ____

2. 8 – 7 = ____

   15 – 14 = ____

3. Circle the ways to make **eleven**.

10 + 1	12 – 2	5 + 6
11 + 0	15 – 4	9 + 1

4. A square has ____ sides.

   A triangle has ____ sides.

5. Four bees flew to three flowers. How many more bees are there than flowers?

   ____ more bee

1. How many squares in all? _____ squares

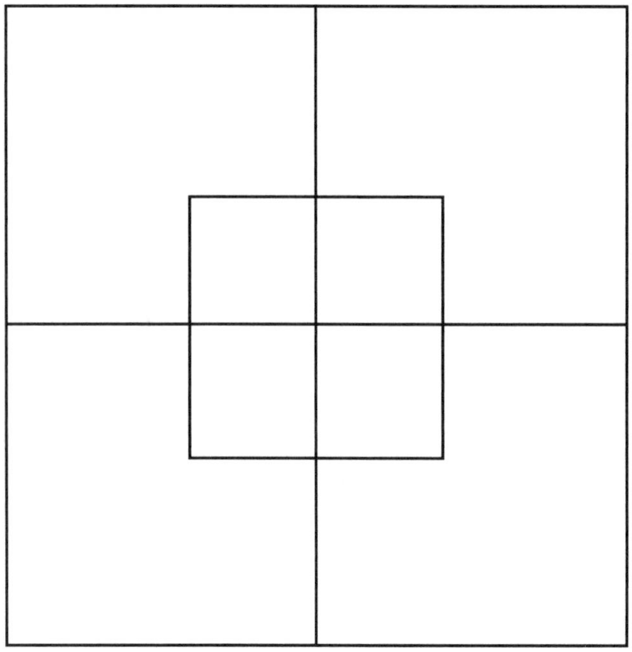

2. How many squares in all? _____ squares

WEEK 19 DAY 1 Daily Math Practice

1 8 + 8 = ____

9 + 9 = ____

2 6 – 3 = ____

8 – 4 = ____

3 Six girls formed two equal teams. How many girls were on each team?

____ girls

4 If 36 + 42 = 78, then

42 + ____ = 78.

5 Color $\frac{1}{2}$ of the rectangle.

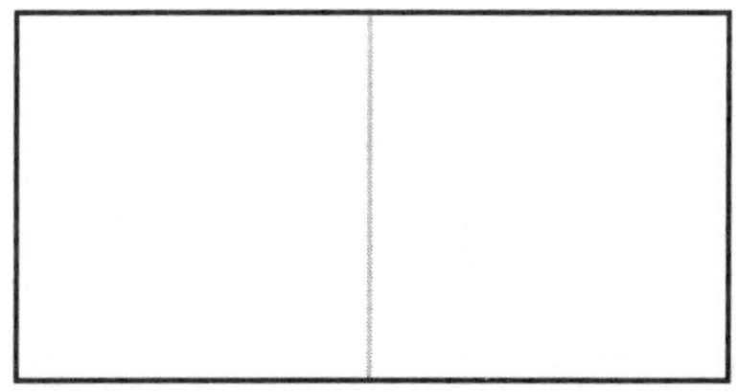

$\frac{1}{2} < 1$ whole

○ **yes** ○ **no**

WEEK 19 DAY 2 Daily Math Practice

1 5 + 5 = ____

6 + 5 = ____

2 12 – 2 = ____

3 Carrie planted three rows of tulips. She put six bulbs in each row. How many bulbs did she plant in all?

____ bulbs

4 Write a subtraction story for the picture.

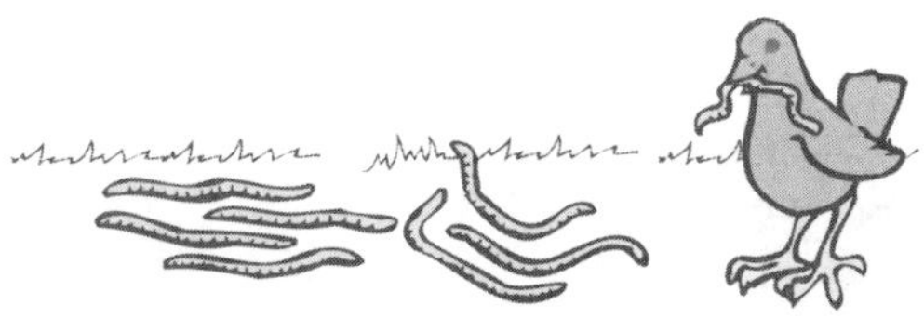

____

____

____

____

5 What is 10 more than 20? ____

1. 13 – 9 = _____

2. How many in all?

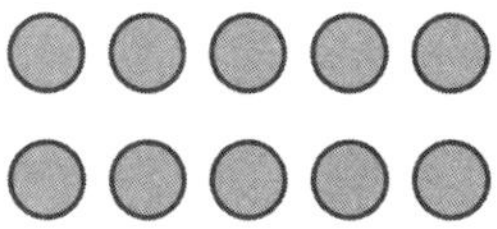 = _____

3. Kendra needs four chairs. She borrowed two from Gavin and two from Tami. How many more chairs does she need?

_____ more chairs

4. $14 = 15$ ○ **yes** ○ **no**

$14 < 15$ ○ **yes** ○ **no**

$14 > 15$ ○ **yes** ○ **no**

5. About how many pounds of potatoes?

1 pound

10 pounds

100 pounds

1. 8 – 1 = 10 – 1

○ **yes** ○ **no**

2. 10 – 5 = _____

20 – 5 = _____

3. Color the squares red.
Color the rectangles yellow.

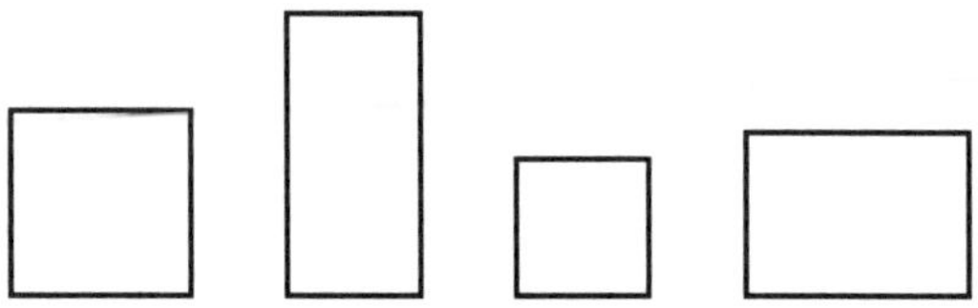

4. Are both sides the same?

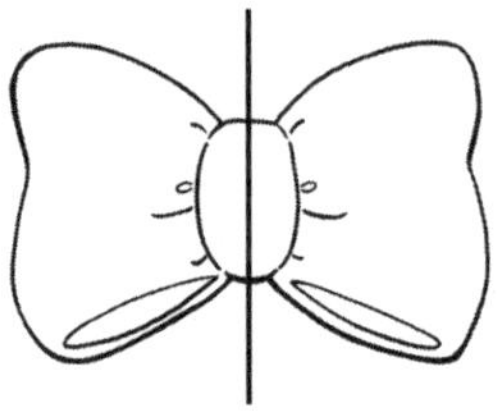

○ **yes** ○ **no**

5. Brad checked out five books and James checked out three books. How many books did they check out altogether?

_____ books

Look at the graph to answer the questions.

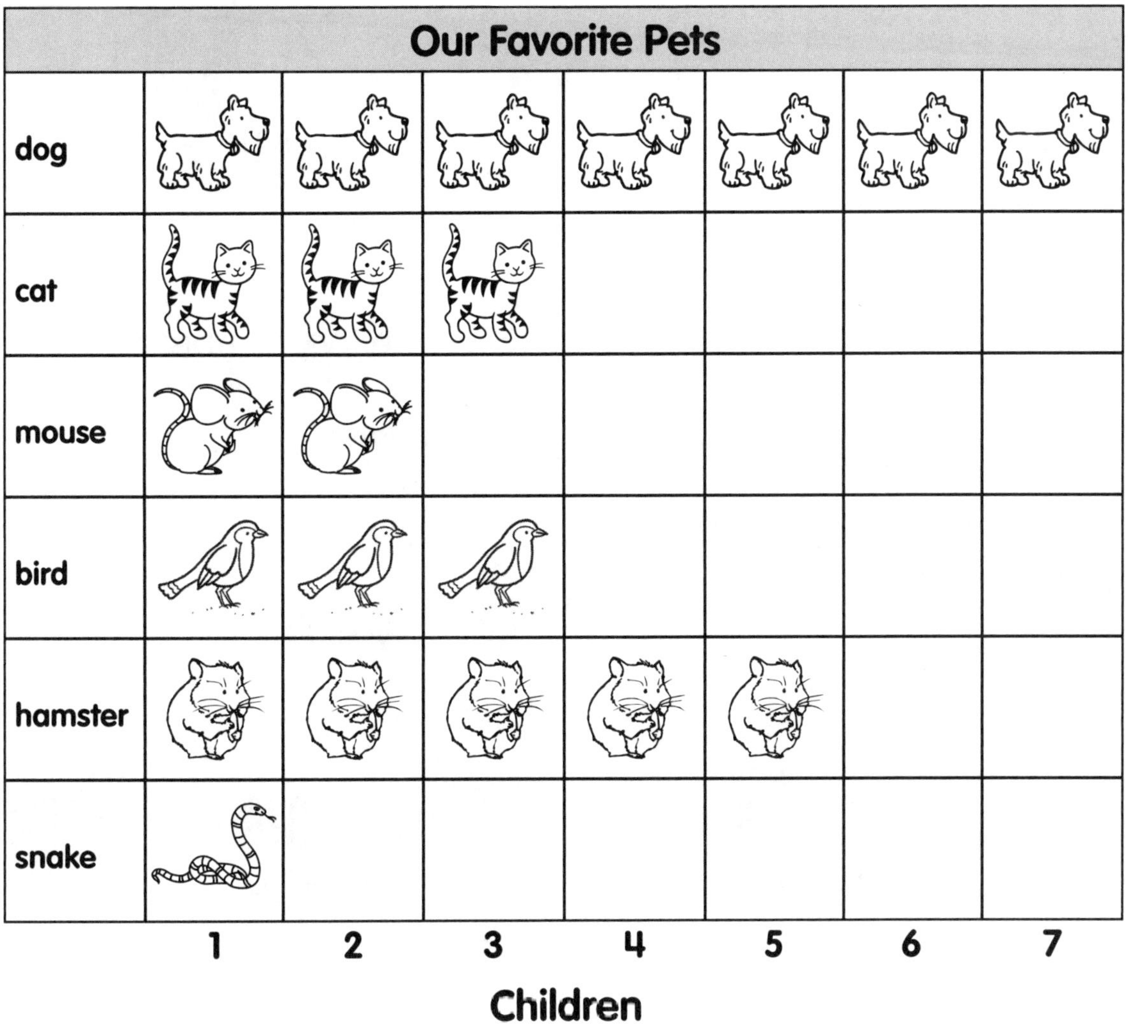

1. Which pet is the most favorite? ______________

2. Which pet is the least favorite? ______________

3. Which **two** pets were picked by the same number of children?

   ______________ and ______________

4. Write something else you learned from the graph.

   ____

   ____

WEEK 20 DAY 1 Daily Math Practice

1 13 − 2 = ____

2 + ____ = 13

2 6 + 10 = ____

7 + 10 = ____

3 Bea made ten cookies. She put three candies on each cookie. How many candies did she use?

____ candies

4 Color $\frac{1}{4}$.

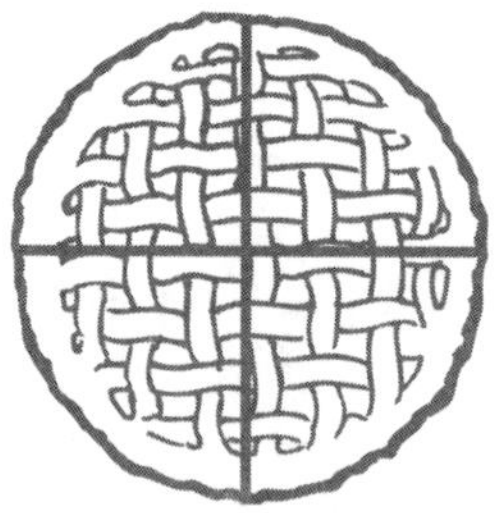

5 Write the numbers.

eleven ____

seventeen ____

thirty-eight ____

WEEK 20 DAY 2 Daily Math Practice

1 4 + 8 = ____

____ − 8 = 4

2 15 − 4 = ____

3 Continue the pattern.

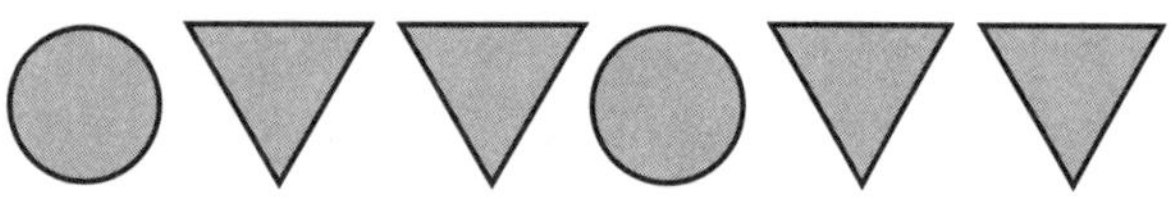

____ ____ ____

4 How many?

____ tally marks

5 The bus had fifteen passengers. Four got off at the first stop. Two got off at the second stop. How many passengers were left?

____ passengers

1 $2 + 9 = 11 + 0$

○ yes ○ no

2 $\begin{array}{r} 8 \\ -\ 6 \\ \hline \end{array}$ $\begin{array}{r} 18 \\ -\ 6 \\ \hline \end{array}$

3 Bob piled blocks in stacks of five. He made six stacks. How many blocks did he use in all?

_____ blocks

4 2 _____ 6 _____ 10 _____ 14

_____ 18 _____

5 Color the cones.

1 $100 + 4 =$ _______

2 $\begin{array}{r} 5 \\ 1 \\ +\ 2 \\ \hline \end{array}$ $\begin{array}{r} 5 \\ +\ 3 \\ \hline \end{array}$

3 Ten balls were in the box. The first graders are using seven of them. How many balls are left?

_____ balls

4 Write the time.

_____ o'clock

5 If $20 + 30 = 50$,

then $50 -$ _____ $= 20$.

1. Doug went fishing. He had 12 worms in a can and 3 in his pocket.

Draw Doug's worms.

2. Doug put a new worm on the hook after every fish he got. He has four worms left. How many fish did he get?

_____ fish

Show your work here.

WEEK 21 DAY 1 Daily Math Practice

1 7 + 10 = ____

17 + 10 = ____

2 6 – 5 = 16 – 15

○ **yes**

○ **no**

3 Rick has two bags of cans to recycle. Joe has three bags. How many bags do they have in all?

____ bags

4 Draw an **X** on the closed figures.

5 Write four number sentences using **6**, **2**, and **8**.

____ + ____ = ____

____ + ____ = ____

____ – ____ = ____

____ – ____ = ____

WEEK 21 DAY 2 Daily Math Practice

1 6 + 7 = ____

7 + 6 = ____

2 3 + 8 + 2 = ____

3 1 ten = ____ 4 tens = ____

2 tens = ____ 5 tens = ____

3 tens = ____ 6 tens = ____

4 Mark the pattern unit.

○ AB ○ ABB ○ AABB

5 Bill walked four blocks to Sam's house, and then he walked back home. How many blocks did he walk in all?

____ blocks

1. 647 + 0 = ______

   647 + 1 = ______

2. 8 + 6 = _____

   18 + 6 = _____

3. Which stem is longer?

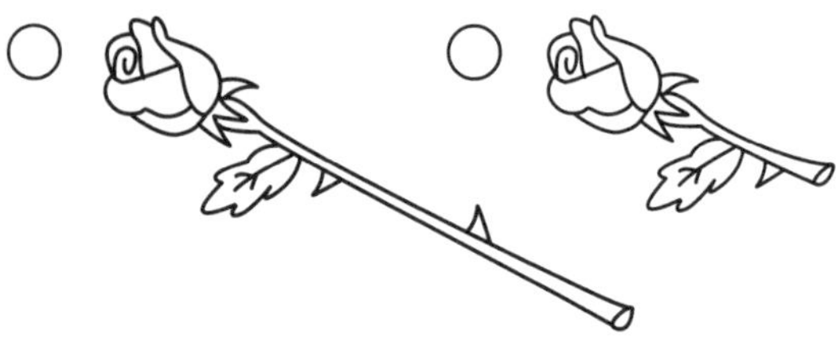

4. If 7 + 3 = 10, then

   _____ – _____ = 7.

5. Tom put three balls, one jump rope, and four beanbags into the bin. How many toys did Tom put into the bin in all?

   _____ toys

1. 8 + 9 = _____

2. 10 – 6 = _____

3. How much?

   _____ cents

4. **Five** is an odd number.

   ○ **yes** ○ **no**

5. Terri and her sister have two bikes and a wagon. How many wheels are there altogether?

   _____ wheels

1. The cook needs one cup of cheese for each pizza. Each package of cheese holds four cups. The class ordered eight pizzas. How many packages of cheese will the cook need?

_____ packages

Show your work here.

2. Mark the pizza that shows fourths.

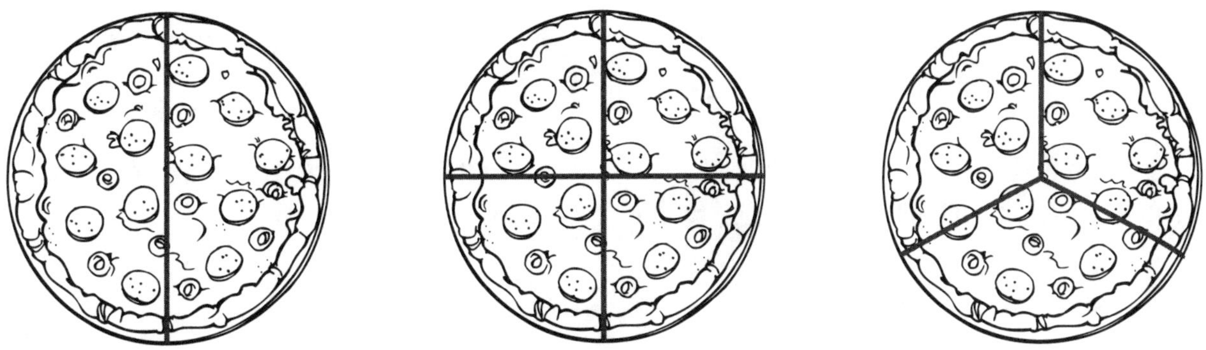

○ ○ ○

WEEK 22 DAY 1 Daily Math Practice

1 50 + 10 = ____

2 10 + 1 = ____

10 + 2 = ____

10 + 3 = ____

3 Draw an **X** on the heaviest.

4 Write the time.

____ o'clock

5 The ball box has two basketballs, three tennis balls, five soccer balls, and one baseball. How many balls are there in all?

____ balls

WEEK 22 DAY 2 Daily Math Practice

1 9 + 3 = ____

____ − 9 = 3

2 23 − 1 = ____

47 − 1 = ____

3 If 6 + 7 = 13, then 13 − ____ = 6.

4 Write 5 more.

20 ____ 40 ____

30 ____ 50 ____

5 Five days in every week are school days. How many days are **not** school days?

____ days

1 1 ten + 6 ones = _____

2 17 – 7 = _____

7 + _____ = 17

3 Chuck planted four trees. One tree died, so he planted another one. How many trees did he plant in all?

_____ trees

4 How much?

_____ cents

5 Circle the ways to make **8**.

5 + 3   2 + 7   4 + 4

6 + 1   8 + 0   16 – 7

1 4 + 7 + 3 = _____

2 10 – 0 = _____   10 – 3 = _____

10 – 1 = _____   10 – 4 = _____

10 – 2 = _____   10 – 5 = _____

3 The fourth mitten has stripes.

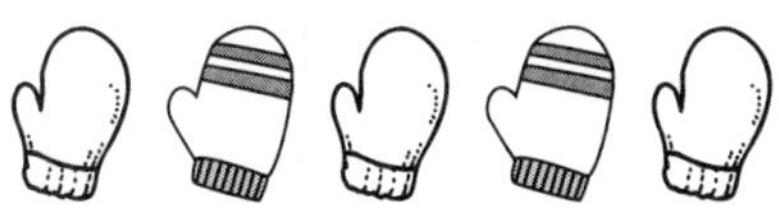

○ **yes**   ○ **no**

4 Circle the straight lines.

5 Cam and Jack took five boxes to the recycling center. The man paid them $1.00. If they share the money equally, how much will each boy get?

_____¢

➤ Activity 1

1. Mark the name of the solid figure.

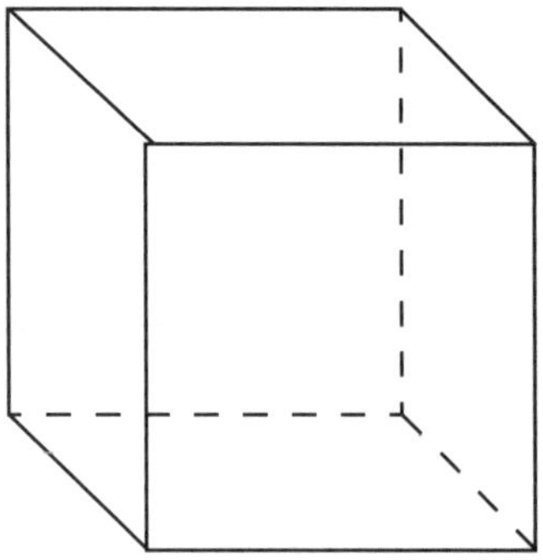

○ cube

○ sphere

○ square

2. How many sides? _____

3. Can it stack? ○ **yes** ○ **no**

4. Can it roll? ○ **yes** ○ **no**

➤ Activity 2

Tess built this stack of cubes.

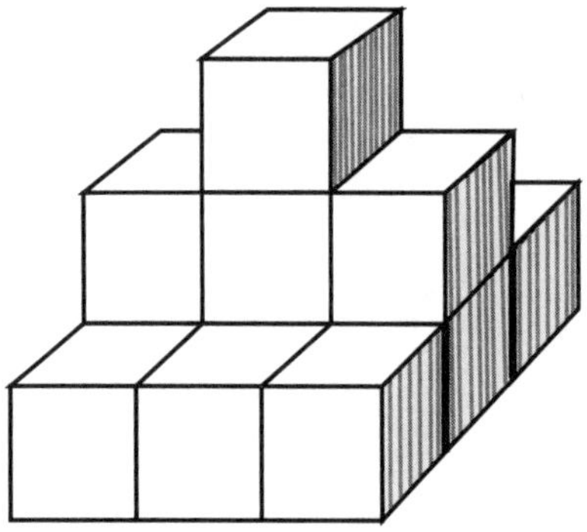

Which drawing shows how the stack looks from the shaded side?

○ 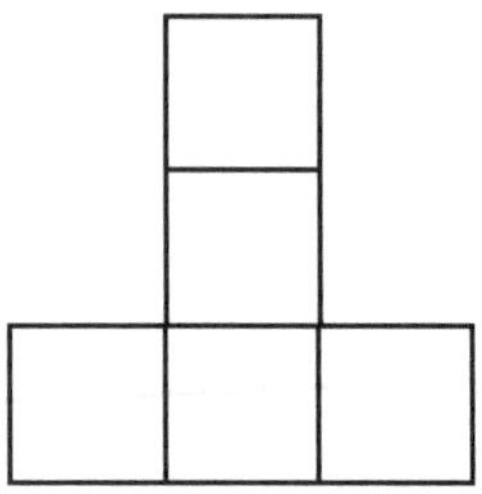

○ 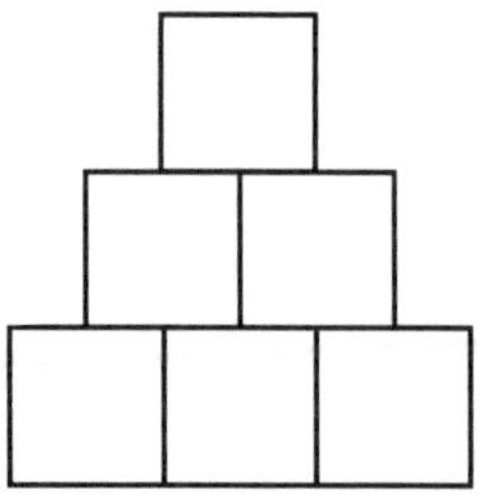

○ 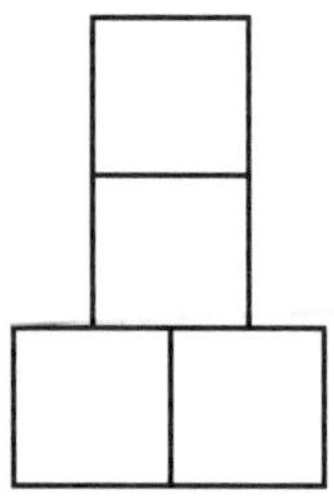

WEEK 23 DAY 1 — Daily Math Practice

1 10 + 8 = _____

12 + 8 = _____

2 8 – 0 = _____

18 – 8 = _____

3 Three birds each laid three eggs. How many eggs are there in all?

_____ eggs

4 Color $\frac{1}{2}$ of all the pigs.

5 Write the number.

zero _____

eight _____

twenty-four _____

forty-two _____

WEEK 23 DAY 2 — Daily Math Practice

1

$$\begin{array}{r} 6 \\ +\ 7 \\ \hline \end{array} \qquad \begin{array}{r} 7 \\ +\ 6 \\ \hline \end{array}$$

2

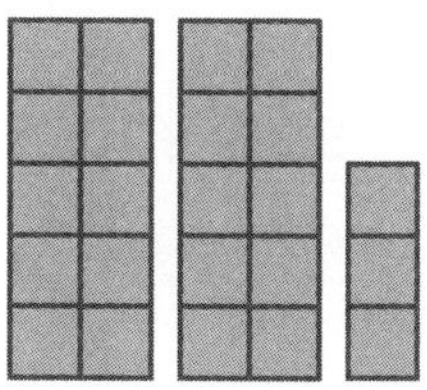

_____ tens + _____ ones = _____

3 Are both sides the same?

○ **yes** ○ **no**

4 Circle the time.

6:30

7:30

8:30

5 Pam gives her dog a bone every morning and every night. How many bones does she give her dog in one week?

_____ bones

1. 9 + 7 = _____

2. How many in all?

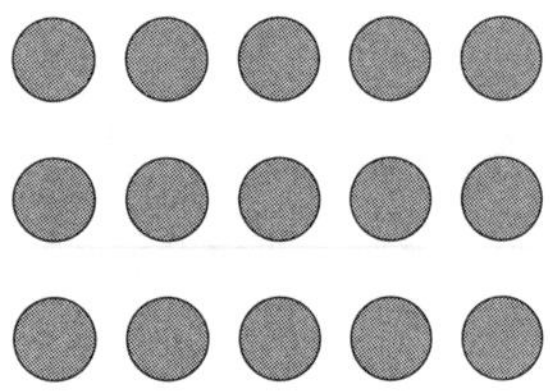

= _____

3. Continue the pattern.

 _____ _____

4. Color the rectangles.

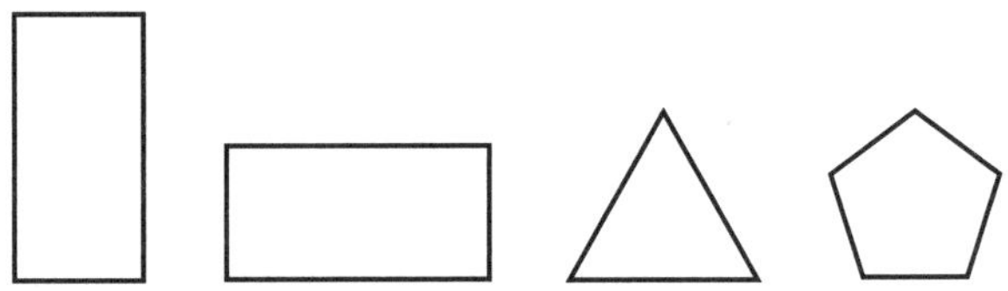

5. The nurse saw 4 boys and 6 girls with colds. How many children did she see in all?

_____ children

1. 15 – 6 = _____

   6 + _____ = 15

2. 2 + 7 + 4 = _____

3. Angela has four pink jelly beans and five purple jelly beans. If she eats three jelly beans, how many will she have left?

   _____ jelly beans

4. 9 + 10 = _____

   10 + 10 = _____

5. Write four number sentences using **2**, **7**, and **9**.

   _____ + _____ = _____

   _____ + _____ = _____

   _____ – _____ = _____

   _____ – _____ = _____

Circle **yes** if both sides are the same.

Circle **no** if both sides are **not** the same.

1.

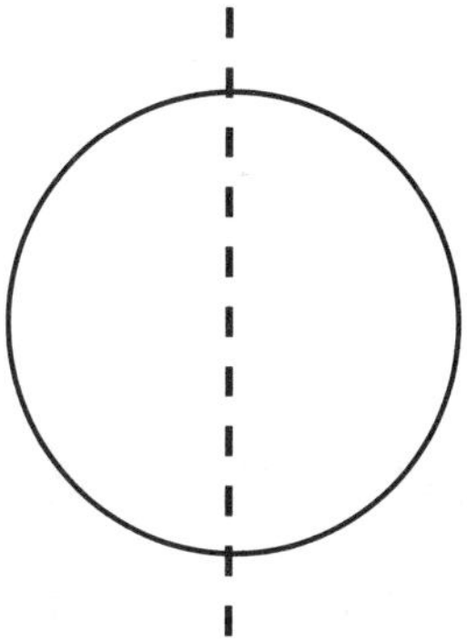

○ **yes** ○ **no**

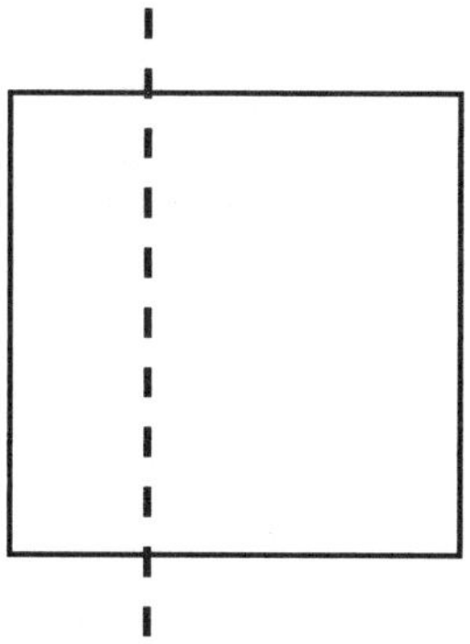

○ **yes** ○ **no**

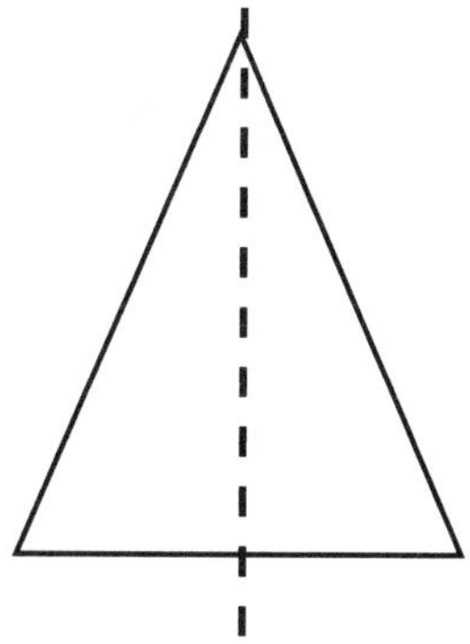

○ **yes** ○ **no**

2.

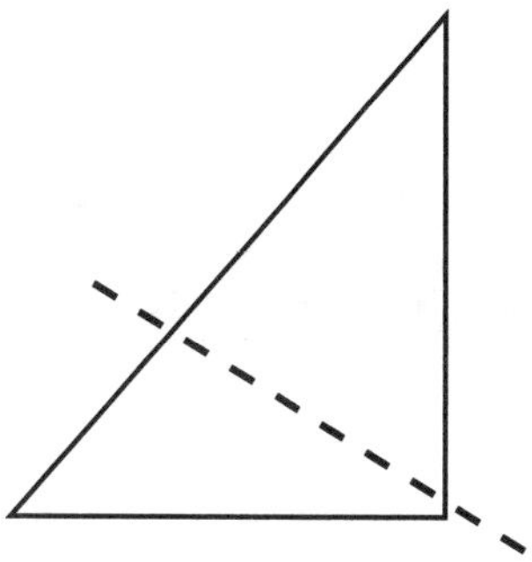

○ **yes** ○ **no**

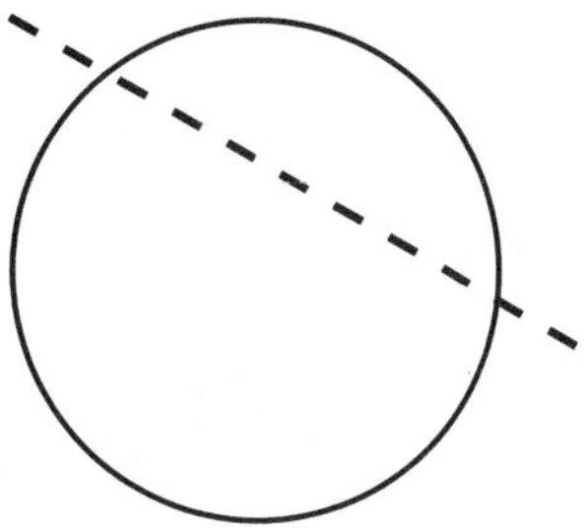

○ **yes** ○ **no**

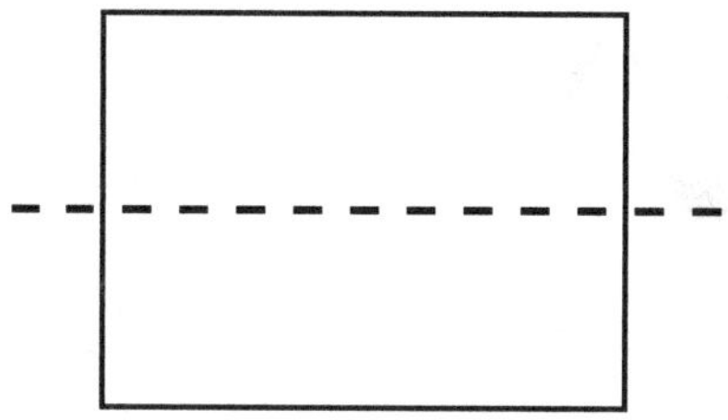

○ **yes** ○ **no**

3.

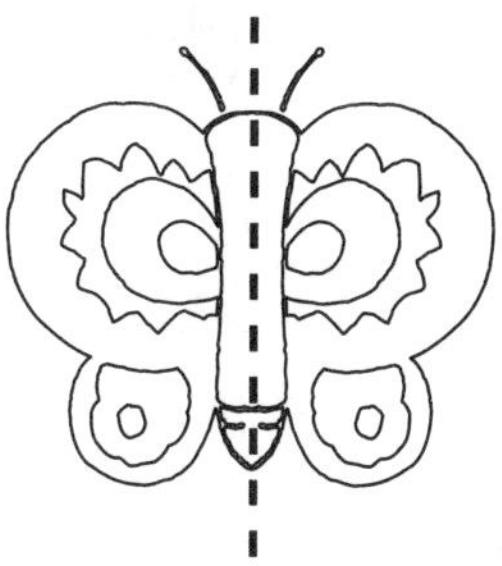

○ **yes** ○ **no**

○ **yes** ○ **no**

○ **yes** ○ **no**

1 7 + 4 = ____

____ − 7 = 4

2 14 − 8 = ____

14 − 10 = ____

3 34 > 31 ○ **yes** ○ **no**

27 > 72 ○ **yes** ○ **no**

4 Color $\frac{1}{4}$ of all the balls.

5 One octopus and two divers are in the water. How many arms are there in all?

____ arms

1 17 = ____ ten + ____ ones

2 18 − 9 = ____

3 The truck holds ten crates, and the driver has loaded six. How many more crates does he need for a full load?

____ crates

4 How many?

____ tally marks

5

ten more
6 ____
30 ____

ten less
____ 39
____ 97

1 9 + 8 = 10 + 7

○ **yes**

○ **no**

2 8 − 3 = ____

____ + 3 = 8

3 Todd has three pencils, four markers, and twenty-two crayons. How many drawing tools does he have?

____ drawing tools

4 Circle the time.

1:00

1:30

6:00

5 If 23 + 5 = 28,

then 28 − ____ = 23.

1 7 + 7 = ____

8 + 8 = ____

2 18 − 5 = ____

3 Two frogs ate six flies. If each frog ate the same number of flies, how many did each frog eat?

____ flies

4 69 < 50 ○ **yes** ○ **no**

47 < 74 ○ **yes** ○ **no**

5 Continue the pattern.

△ ○ ○ □ △ ○ ○ □

____ ____ ____ ____

Each group of students planted ten seeds. Each seed can make one sprout. How many sprouting seeds did each group have?

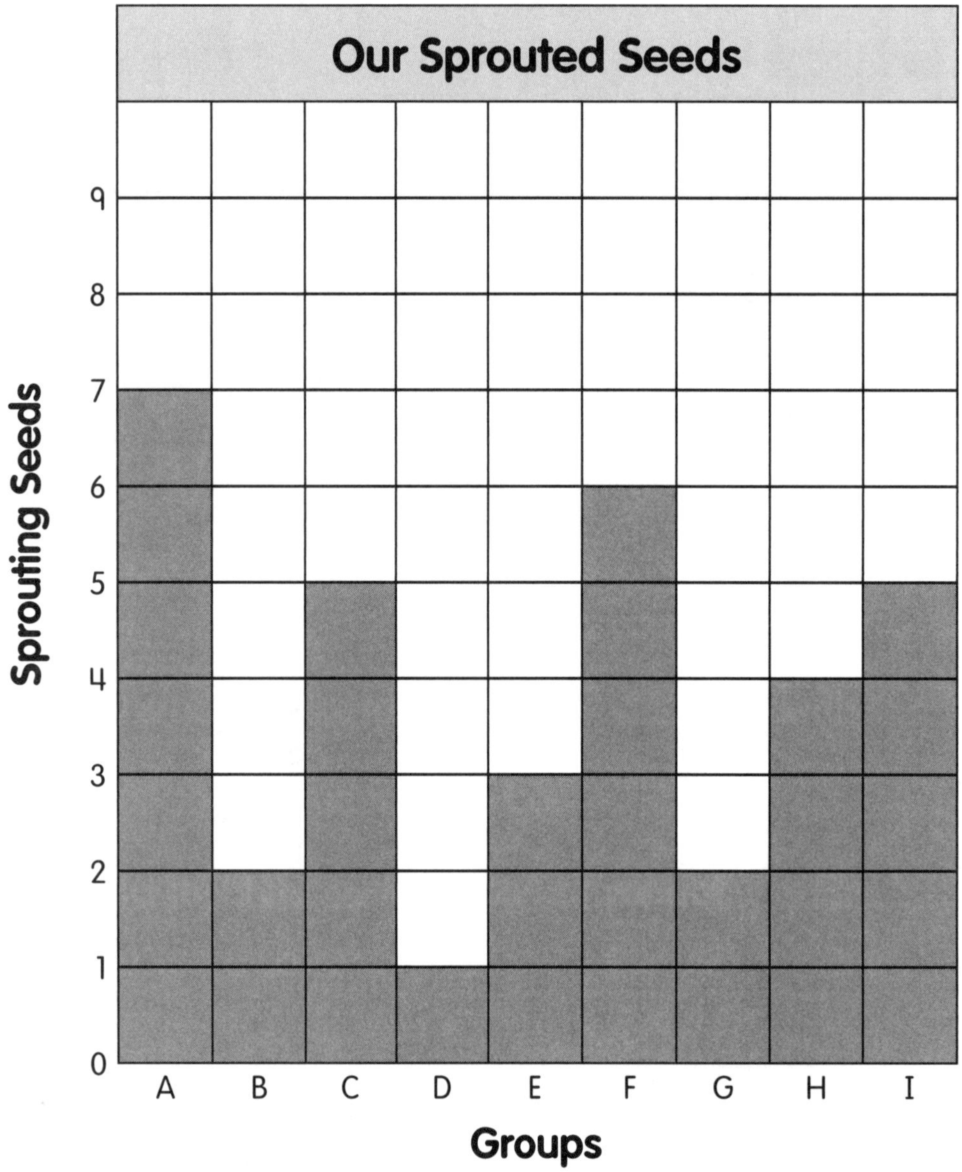

Group A _____ Group B _____ Group C _____

Group D _____ Group E _____ Group F _____

Group G _____ Group H _____ Group I _____

1

$$\begin{array}{r} 9 \\ -\ 5 \\ \hline \end{array} \qquad \begin{array}{r} 19 \\ -\ 5 \\ \hline \end{array}$$

2 Luke has two boards. He needs four nails for each board. How many nails does he need?

_____ nails

3

$$\begin{array}{r} 6 \\ +\ 5 \\ \hline \end{array} \qquad \begin{array}{r} 8 \\ +\ 7 \\ \hline \end{array} \qquad \begin{array}{r} 9 \\ +\ 8 \\ \hline \end{array}$$

4 How much?

_____ cents

5 65 64 63 _____ _____ _____

_____ _____ _____ _____ _____

1 2 + 4 – 2 + 1 = _____

2 Mark the pattern unit.

△△□○△△□○

○ AAB ○ AABC ○ ABC

3 If 5 + 23 = 28,

then 23 + 5 = _____.

4 Color the half circles.

5 There are six books on the table, three books on the chair, and ten books on the shelf. How many books are there in all?

_____ books

1. 3 + 7 = _____

2. 8,247 + 0 = ________

3. Show four ways to make **12**.

_____ + _____ = 12

_____ + _____ = 12

_____ − _____ = 12

_____ − _____ = 12

4. Draw an **X** on the line that is 2 paper clips long.

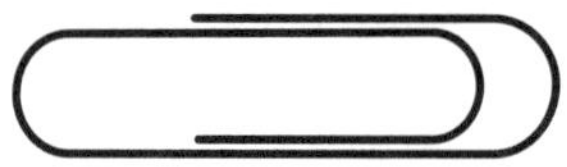

A __________

B ________________________________

C _________________

5. **6** is an odd number.

○ **yes** ○ **no**

1. 17 − 9 = _____

2.
$$\begin{array}{r} 7 \\ 6 \\ +\ 4 \\ \hline \end{array} \qquad \begin{array}{r} 7 \\ +\ 10 \\ \hline \end{array}$$

3. Scott put six books, three pencils, and a notebook in his backpack. How many school supplies are in his backpack?

_____ school supplies

4. 100 + 10 + 9 = ?

○ 100 ○ 119 ○ 19

5. How long is the gum?

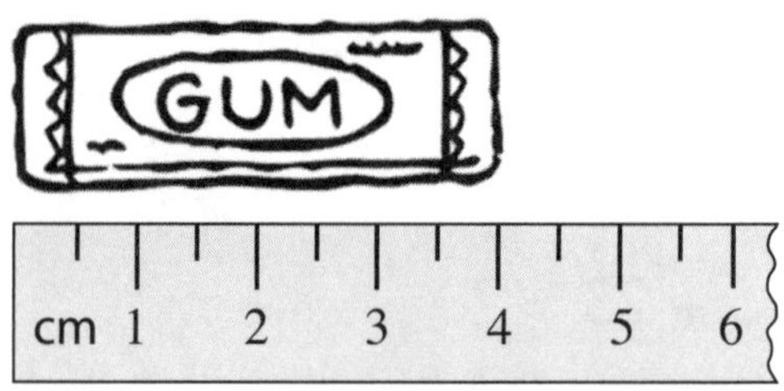

_____ centimeters

Activity 1

What does **not** belong? Draw an **X** on it.

Tell how the other things are alike.

____

____

Activity 2

The dog ate my 100s chart!

Write the missing numbers.

		49	50
	58		
67			70
	78		

1 9 + 10 = ____

10 + 10 = ____

2 16 – 8 = ____

8 + ____ = 16

3 20 ____ ____ 35

____ 45 ____

4 Circle the second star.

5 The ship has four red flags, seven green flags, and three yellow flags. How many flags does the ship have in all?

____ flags

1 8 + 5 = ____

2 9 + 6 = ____

3 Write **<** or **>** to tell the rule:

Group A
1, 4, 3, 6, 2, 5

All numbers are ____ 7.

Group B
8, 10, 9, 11, 13, 12

All numbers are ____ 7.

4 Draw an **X** on the heaviest.

5 Each lunch bag has two sandwiches in it. How many sandwiches are in six bags?

____ sandwiches

1. 13 – 4 = ____

   13 – 3 = ____

2. If 41 + 8 = ____, then

   ____ – 8 = 41.

3. The ladder has 18 rungs. Tom climbed halfway up. How many rungs did he climb?

   ____ rungs

4. 2 + 20 = ____ 4 + 20 = ____

   3 + 20 = ____ 5 + 20 = ____

5. Color the circle green.
   Color the triangle black.
   Color the square pink.

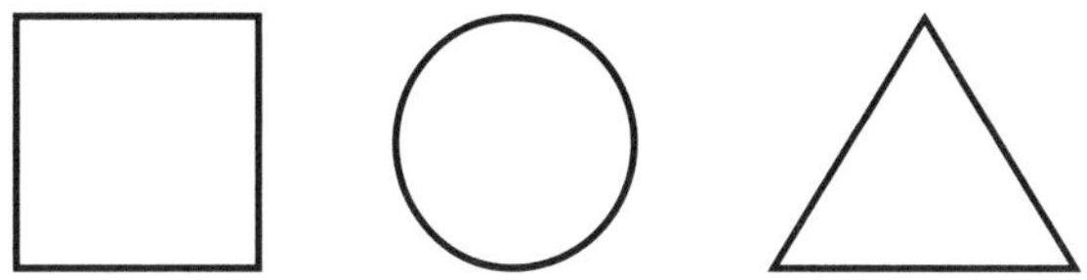

1. 17 – 8 = ____

   8 + ____ = 17

2. 10 + 9 = ____

3. Mark the name for the shaded part.

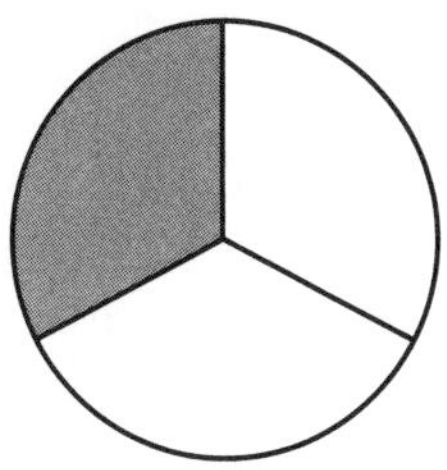

○ $\frac{1}{4}$

○ $\frac{1}{3}$

○ $\frac{1}{2}$

4. Five boys and seven girls sat in a row. Write a number sentence about the row.

   ____ + ____ = ____

5. Circle the ways to make **9**.

8 + 1	7 – 2	3 + 6
5 + 4	9 – 0	12 – 3

1. The soccer team scored four goals in their first game, five goals in their second game, and two goals in their third game. How many goals did they score in all?

_____ goals

Show your work here.

2. The team lost the third game. At least how many goals did the other team score?

_____ goals

Show your work here.

1 18 + 4 = ____

____ – 18 = 4

2 6 + 8 = ____

____ – 6 = 8

3 Troy has 3 yellow cars, 7 green cars, and 6 white cars. How many cars does he have in all?

____ cars

4

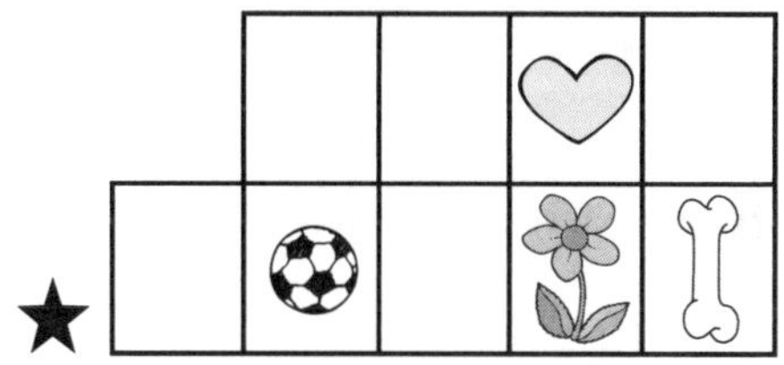

Start at the star. Which answer tells how to find the ball?

○ left 2 boxes ○ right 2 boxes

5 Write the number.

fifteen ____ sixty ____

fifty ____

1 7 + 3 = ____

17 + 3 = ____

2 12 – 7 = ____

7 + ____ = 12

3 Harry caught two ants, three crickets, and six beetles. How many bugs did he catch in all?

____ bugs

4 $8 < 18$ ○ **yes** ○ **no**

$24 > 42$ ○ **yes** ○ **no**

5 About how many cans of apple juice?

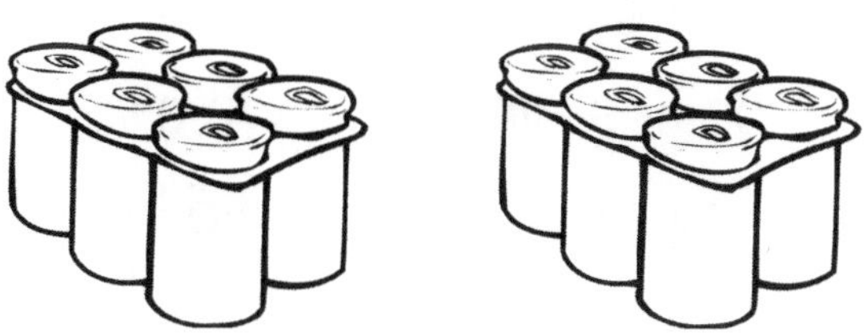

6 12 18

WEEK 27 DAY 3 Daily Math Practice

1. 6 + 9 = ____

   9 + 6 = ____

2. 20 – 10 = ____

   30 – 10 = ____

3. Tim took four cookies. If he ate half of them, how many cookies did he eat?

   ____ cookies

4. Write a story problem for **6 – 2 = ?**

   ____

   ____

   ____

   ____

5. 5 + 4 = ____ + ____

   23 + 21 = ____ + ____

WEEK 27 DAY 4 Daily Math Practice

1. 7 + 8 = 10 + 5

   ○ **yes** ○ **no**

2. 17 – 8 = ____

3. Scott ate six pretzels, three cookies, and a brownie. How many snacks did he eat in all?

   ____ snacks

4. Write four number sentences using **6**, **9**, and **15**.

   ____ + ____ = ____

   ____ + ____ = ____

   ____ – ____ = ____

   ____ – ____ = ____

5. Are both sides the same?

   ○ **yes** ○ **no**

➤ Activity 1

Match the pattern to its name.

• ABC

• AB

• AAB

➤ Activity 2

Show ways to make **15**. Use **+** and **–**.

____ ○ ____ = 15 ____ ○ ____ = 15

____ ○ ____ = 15 ____ ○ ____ = 15

____ ○ ____ = 15 ____ ○ ____ = 15

____ ○ ____ = 15 ____ ○ ____ = 15

____ ○ ____ = 15 ____ ○ ____ = 15

WEEK 28 DAY 1 Daily Math Practice

1

$$\begin{array}{r} 13 \\ -\ 5 \\ \hline \end{array} \qquad \begin{array}{r} 15 \\ -\ 5 \\ \hline \end{array}$$

2 Count by 2s.

20 22 24 ____ ____

____ ____ ____ ____

3

$$\begin{array}{r} 12 \\ +\ 2 \\ \hline \end{array}$$

The sum is an even number.

○ **yes** ○ **no**

4 Write the number.

ninety-one ____

sixty-four ____

5 John ate $\frac{1}{2}$ of his sandwich for lunch and $\frac{1}{2}$ of his sandwich for a snack after school. How much is left?

________ is left

WEEK 28 DAY 2 Daily Math Practice

1 6 + 3 + 2 = ____

2 30 + 40 = ____

35 + 40 = ____

3 What comes next?

○ △ △ ○ △ △ ○ ____

 ____

4 How many?

____ tally marks

5 Juan had 105 marbles. His friend gave him 10 more. How many marbles does Juan have now?

______ marbles

WEEK 28 DAY 3 Daily Math Practice

1. 4 + 7 = _____

   11 − 7 = _____

2. 15 + 6 = _____

3. Circle the time.

5:00   12:00   5:30

4. If 17 + 4 = 21, then 21 − 4 = _____.

5. Mr. Brown asked 5 students to each bring 2 books they had read to the PTA meeting. How many books did they bring in all?

   _____ books

WEEK 28 DAY 4 Daily Math Practice

1. 9 + 5 = _____

2. 15 + 0 = _____

3. Write a number sentence.

_____ ◯ _____ = _____

4. Six cars were parked in the first row. Seven cars were parked in the second row. Five cars were parked in the third row. Which row had the most cars?

   ○ first ○ second ○ third

5. $8 > 6$ ○ **yes** ○ **no**

➤ Activity 1

Our Favorite Ice Cream Each scoop = 1 student

vanilla | chocolate | mint | rocky road | butter pecan | strawberry

1. How many students like ice cream? _____ students
2. Which flavor do the students like best? ____________________
3. Do more students like butter pecan or vanilla? ____________________
4. Which flavor is your favorite? ____________________

➤ Activity 2

Write the missing numbers.

	2								10
							18		
			24						
									40

WEEK 29 DAY 1 Daily Math Practice

1 6 + 5 = _____

5 + 6 = _____

2 14 – 5 = _____

3 Sara's window has four corners and four equal sides. What shape is Sara's window?

○ triangle

○ square

○ rectangle

4 How much?

_____ cents

5 Circle the even numbers.

1 2 3 4 5 6 7 8

WEEK 29 DAY 2 Daily Math Practice

1 8 + 7 = _____

2

$$\begin{array}{r} 11 \\ +\ 3 \\ \hline \end{array} \qquad \begin{array}{r} 12 \\ +\ 2 \\ \hline \end{array}$$

3 Tessa has four brothers and two sisters. How many children are in Tessa's family?

_____ children

4 Which is longer?

○ one inch ○ one foot

5 Write a story for **7 – 5 = ?**

____

____

____

____

1 100 – 10 = ____

2 16 = ____ ten + ____ ones

40 = ____ tens + ____ ones

3 Carly sold three boxes of candy. Seth sold seven boxes. How many boxes did they sell altogether?

____ boxes

4 Circle the shapes that have more than three sides.

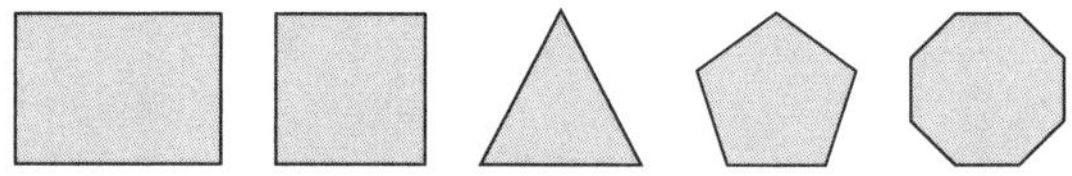

5

Add 10			
2		5	
3		6	
4		7	

1 19 + 10 = ____

2 20 + 40 + 10 = ____

3 If Tina has ten puppies and four leashes, how many puppies do **not** have leashes?

____ puppies

4 Write four number sentences using **10**, **11**, and **21**.

____ + ____ = ____

____ + ____ = ____

____ – ____ = ____

____ – ____ = ____

5 $\begin{array}{r} 8 \\ +\ 9 \\ \hline \end{array}$ $\begin{array}{r} 9 \\ +\ 8 \\ \hline \end{array}$

Activity 1

Each student needs two pencils and a ruler to do a project. If there are six students, how many pencils do they need altogether?

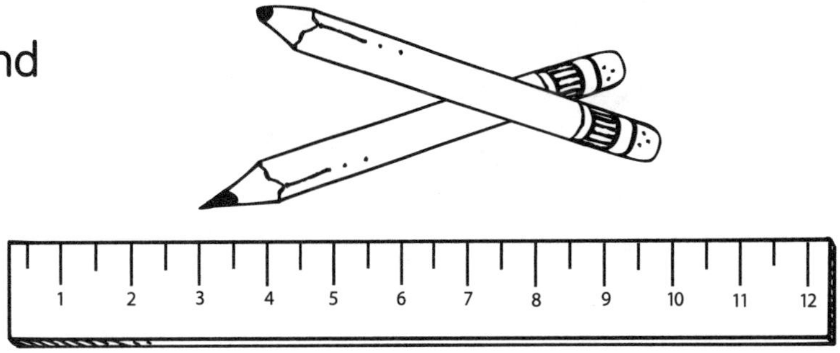

_____ pencils

How many rulers do they need altogether?

_____ rulers

Show your work.

Activity 2

2 + 2 + 2 + 2 + 2 + 2 = _____

5 + 5 + 5 + 5 = _____

10 + 10 + 10 + 10 + 10 = _____

1 Draw an **X** on the sixth pin.

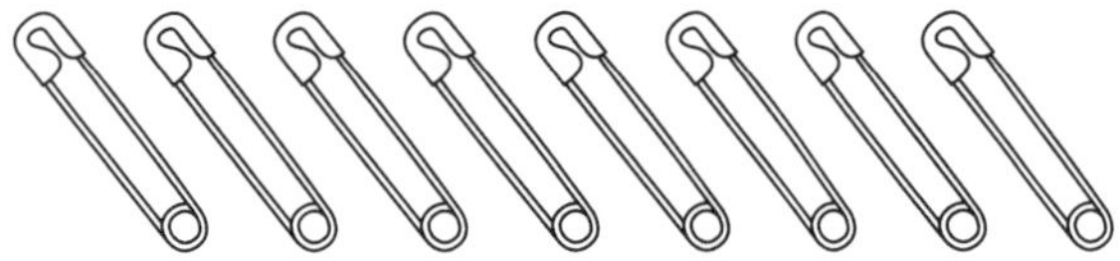

2

$$\begin{array}{r} 4 \\ +\ 8 \\ \hline \end{array} \qquad \begin{array}{r} 6 \\ +\ 8 \\ \hline \end{array} \qquad \begin{array}{r} 8 \\ +\ 8 \\ \hline \end{array}$$

3 How many letters are in Stephanie's name?

_____ letters

4 25 30 35 _____ _____

_____ _____ _____ _____

5 5 + 5 = _____

6 + 6 = _____

7 + 7 = _____

8 + 8 = _____

9 + 9 = _____

1 9 + 2 = _____

10 + 2 = _____

2 16 – 4 = _____

4 + _____ = 16

3 Eight coconuts were on the tree. Three fell off. How many are left?

_____ coconuts

4 Write the time.

_____ o'clock

5 Color the beads. Make the spheres green. Make the cubes purple.

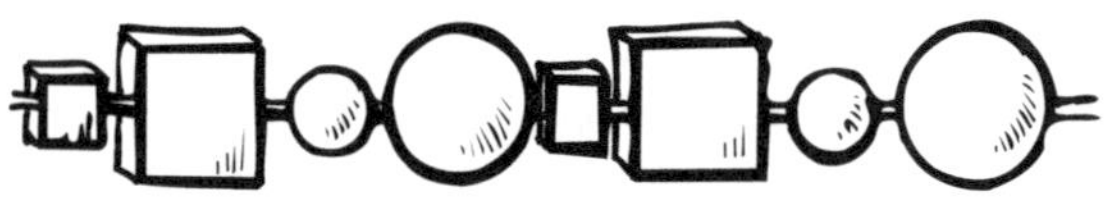

1 17 – 8 = _____

2
```
  5      2
  5      2
+ 5    + 2
```

3 Minnie likes even numbers. Mickey likes odd numbers. Who likes **7**?

○ Minnie ○ Mickey

4 Write an addition number sentence.

_____ + _____ + _____ = _____

5 Is 40 pounds heavier than 30 pounds?

○ **yes** ○ **no**

1 7 + 5 = 11 + 1 ○ **yes** ○ **no**

2 25 – 5 = _____

5 + _____ = 25

3 There are four plates, four cups, and four forks on the table. How many people can eat?

_____ people

4 Show four ways to make **16**.

_____ + _____ = 16

_____ + _____ = 16

_____ – _____ = 16

_____ – _____ = 16

5 If 8 + 9 = 17,

then _____ = 9 + _____.

➤ Activity 1

I put six pretzels, four candies, and two cookies in my snack bag. How many things do I have in all?

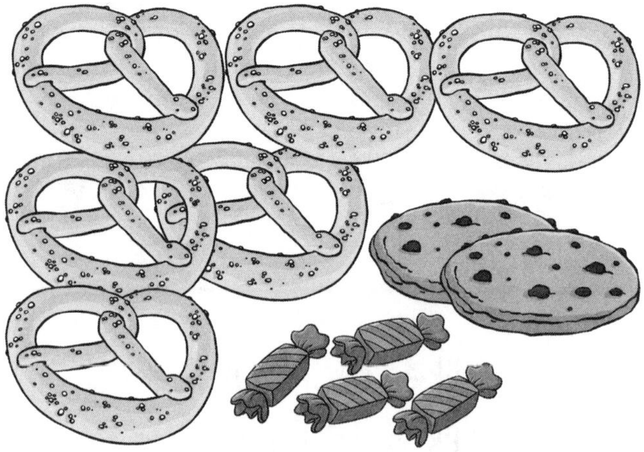

_____ things

If I eat the pretzels, how many things will I have left?

_____ things

Show your work.

➤ Activity 2

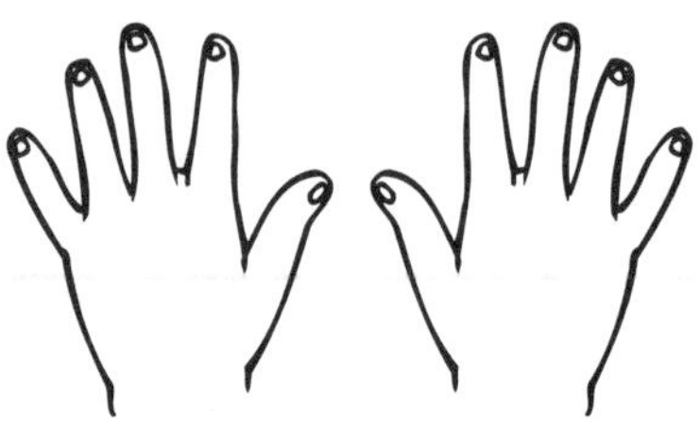

Circle the left hand.

Draw an **X** on the right hand.

1 $6 + 4 = 7 + 3$ ○ yes ○ no

2 $5 + 6 =$ ____

$15 + 6 =$ ____

3 Tim had six paper clips. He used two on a puppet and two on a book. How many paper clips did he have left?

____ paper clips

4 Color $\frac{1}{3}$ of all the pockets.

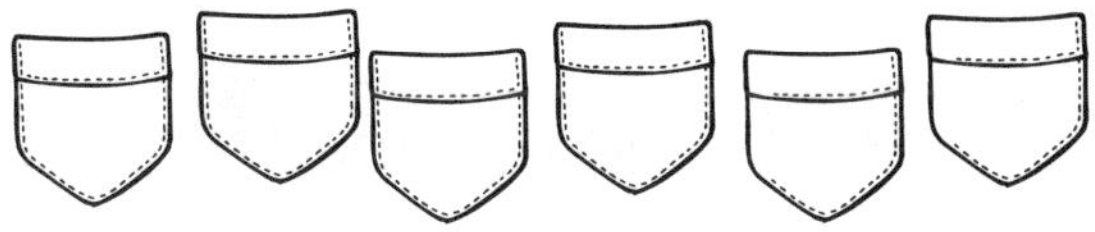

5 Match the words and numbers.

2	five	5
	three	
3	six	6
	four	
4	seven	7
	two	

1
$$\begin{array}{r} 42 \\ -\ 2 \\ \hline \end{array} \qquad \begin{array}{r} 67 \\ -\ 5 \\ \hline \end{array}$$

2
$$\begin{array}{r} 341 \\ +\ 23 \\ \hline \end{array} \qquad \begin{array}{r} 404 \\ +\ 32 \\ \hline \end{array}$$

3 Seven bees flew to four flowers. How many more bees than flowers were there?

____ more bees

4 About how many toothpicks?

10 100 1,000

5 $9 < 9$ ○ yes ○ no

$9 > 9$ ○ yes ○ no

$9 = 9$ ○ yes ○ no

WEEK 31 DAY 3 Daily Math Practice

1. 16 – 8 = _____

2. Match each shape to its name.

square circle triangle rectangle

3. Liz put six black beads and six brown beads on her necklace. How many beads did she use in all?

   _____ beads

4. Circle the ways to make **18**.

   18 + 0   17 + 2   15 + 3

5. Three girls played jump rope. Four boys played tag. Six other children played four square. How many children played in all?

   ○ 3 + 4 = 7

   ○ 3 + 4 + 6 = 17

   ○ 3 + 4 + 6 = 13

WEEK 31 DAY 4 Daily Math Practice

1. Continue the pattern.

   1 3 5 7 _____ _____ _____

2. 4 + 7 + 2 = _____

3. Ava wants to fill a planter box. It holds five bags of soil. If Ava has two bags, how many more does she need?

   _____ more bags

4. 15 – 5 = _____   25 – 5 = _____

   16 – 6 = _____   26 – 6 = _____

   17 – 7 = _____   27 – 7 = _____

5. Are the sides the same?

   ○ **yes**

   ○ **no**

Activity 1

Show eight different ways to color the circles.
Use only red and blue. Plan before you color.

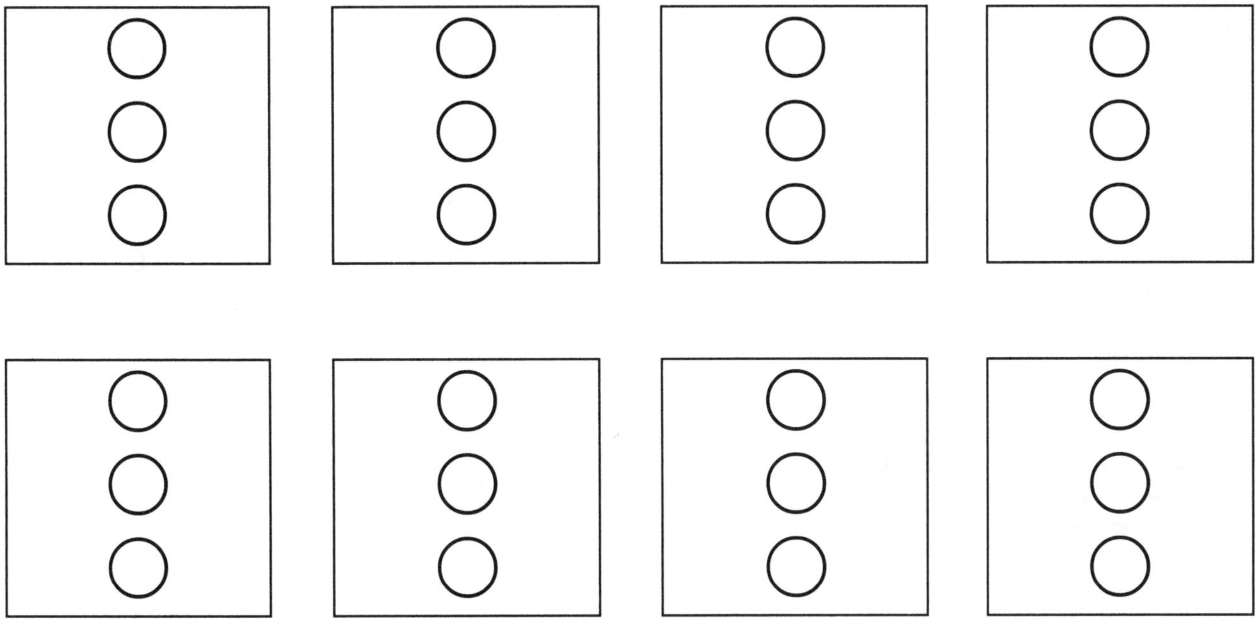

Activity 2

Rosa made a tower using four blocks as the base, three blocks for the next two levels, and one block on the top. How many blocks are in the tower?

_____ blocks

Draw the tower.

WEEK 32 DAY 1 Daily Math Practice

1. $67 - 52 =$ _____

2.
$$\begin{array}{r} 42 \\ 31 \\ +15 \\ \hline \end{array} \qquad \begin{array}{r} 23 \\ 51 \\ +22 \\ \hline \end{array}$$

3. Write the time.

half past _____

4. If $54 + 32 = 86$,

then _____ $- 32 =$ _____.

5. Drew needs a new pair of pants. He has \$10.00. If the pants cost \$8.00, how much change will he get?

\$________

WEEK 32 DAY 2 Daily Math Practice

1. $4 + 2 + 7 + 1 =$ _____

2. $5 + 3 - 2 =$ _____

3. Claire made a dozen cookies for her 6 friends. She will give the same number of cookies to each friend. How many will each friend get?

_____ cookies

4. Mark the name for the shaded part.

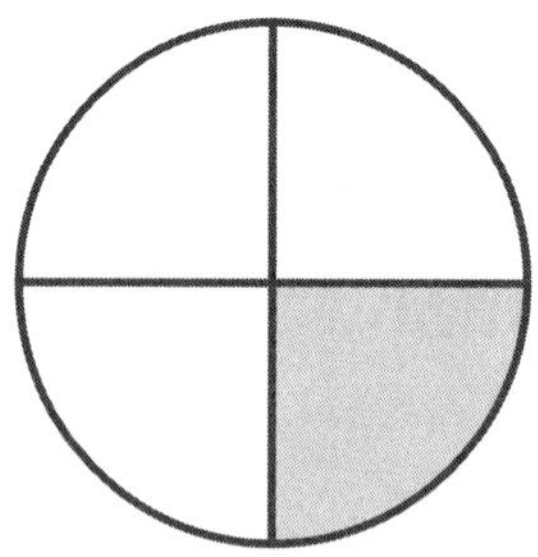

○ $\frac{1}{3}$

○ $\frac{2}{4}$

○ $\frac{1}{4}$

5. Write the number.

one hundred ______

1. 18 – 7 = ____

   7 + ____ = 18

2. 15 + 13 = ____

   28 – 15 = ____

3. 2 4 6 ____ ____ ____

   2 + 2 + 2 + 2 + 2 + 2 = ____

4. 647 < 532 ○ **yes** ○ **no**

   209 > 199 ○ **yes** ○ **no**

5. Cindy has four nickels in her purse and two nickels in her pocket. How many nickels does she have in all?

   ____ nickels

   How much are they worth?

   ____¢

1. 3 + 4 + 9 = ____

2. 9 – 2 – 3 = ____

3. Color the rectangles.

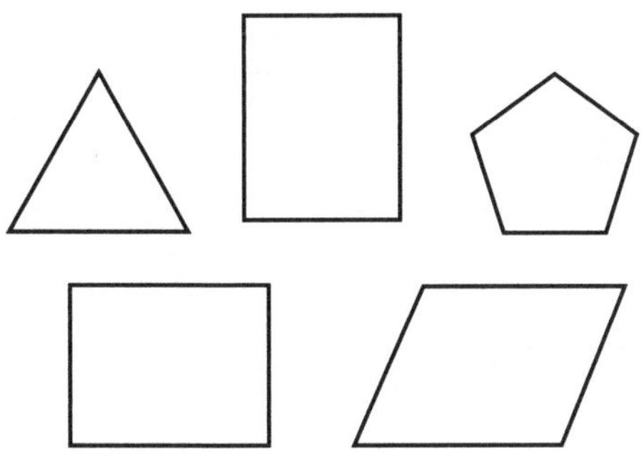

4. How many?

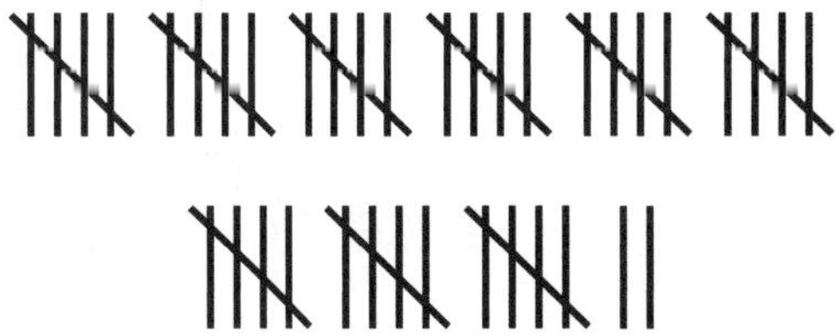

   ____ tally marks

5. Five frogs each ate five flies. How many flies did the frogs eat in all?

   ____ flies

1. Count the letters in each name: **Lakesha**, **Teyo**, **Emily**, **Ayden**, **Jon**. Color the boxes on the graph to show the number of letters for each name.

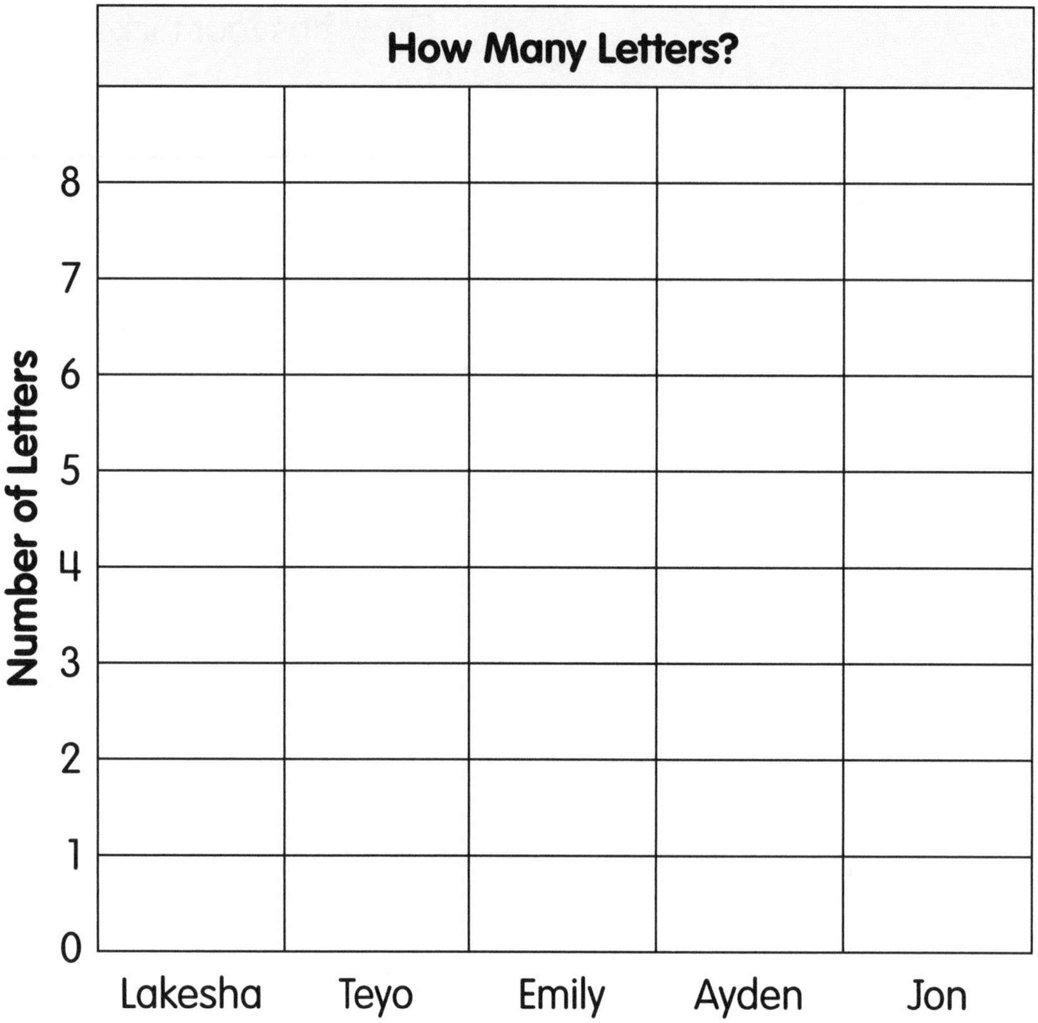

2. Write something you learned from the graph.

____

____

____

1. 5 + 8 = ____

   ____ − 5 = 8

2. 14 − 9 = ____

   24 − 9 = ____

3. The fish tank has 6 guppies, 7 zebra fish, 1 catfish, and 1 snail. How many animals are in the fish tank?

   ____ animals

4. How much?

= ____ cents

= ____ cents

= ____ cents

5. 6 + 2 + 1 + 0 = ____

1. 17 − 7 = ____

   17 − 8 = ____

   17 − 9 = ____

2. 14 + 6 = ____

3. 50 60 70 ____ ____

   ____ ____ ____

4. Mark the pattern unit.

○ ABAC ○ ABAB ○ ABCA

5. The number is **73**.

   How many tens? ____

   How many ones? ____

WEEK 33 DAY 3 Daily Math Practice

1

$$\begin{array}{r} 8 \\ -\ 2 \\ \hline \end{array} \qquad \begin{array}{r} 18 \\ -\ 2 \\ \hline \end{array}$$

2

$$\begin{array}{r} 7 \\ 1 \\ +\ 5 \\ \hline \end{array} \qquad \begin{array}{r} 8 \\ +\ 5 \\ \hline \end{array}$$

3 Circle the ways to make **6**.

3 + 3   7 – 1   2 + 5

4 + 3   5 + 1   8 – 3

4 84 = _____ tens + _____ ones

70 = _____ tens + _____ ones

55 = _____ tens + _____ ones

5 Dave found four eggs in a nest and five eggs in a basket. How many eggs did he find in all?

_____ eggs

WEEK 33 DAY 4 Daily Math Practice

1 8 + 9 = _____

9 + 8 = _____

2 18 – 6 = _____

6 + _____ = 18

3 **32** is an odd number.

○ **yes**   ○ **no**

4 Color the figures with four corners and four sides.

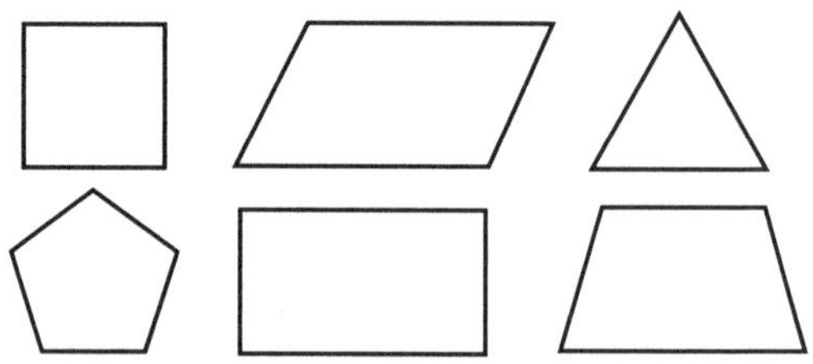

5 Mia and Jo each picked four flowers. They put three in a vase. How many flowers are left?

_____ flowers

Activity 1

Jesse cut out three hearts, six circles, and three squares.

He made an **ABBC** repeating pattern using all the shapes.

Draw **two** patterns he could have made.

Activity 2

Draw an **ABCB** repeating pattern. Use triangles, rectangles, and circles.

1

$$\begin{array}{r} 52 \\ -41 \\ \hline \end{array} \qquad \begin{array}{r} 74 \\ -23 \\ \hline \end{array}$$

2

$$\begin{array}{r} 37 \\ +41 \\ \hline \end{array} \qquad \begin{array}{r} 85 \\ +12 \\ \hline \end{array}$$

3 Erik ate five pieces of pizza. If the pizza was cut into eight pieces, how many are left?

_____ pieces

4 Draw an **X** on the tenth banana.

5 10 + 2 = ?

Circle the correct answers.

4 + 8

11 + 0

9 + 3

1 Two pounds > $\frac{1}{2}$ pound.

○ **yes** ○ **no**

2

$$\begin{array}{r} 73 \\ 14 \\ +12 \\ \hline \end{array} \qquad \begin{array}{r} 51 \\ 23 \\ +15 \\ \hline \end{array}$$

3 5 10 15 _____ _____ _____

_____ _____ _____ _____

4 Circle the clock that shows half past six.

5 Six kids each make two piles of sand. How many piles of sand are there in all?

_____ piles

1 943 – 10 = ______

2 Circle the even numbers.

3 8 1 6 4 2 9

3 7 + 10 = _____

6 + 10 = _____

7 + 100 = ______

6 + 100 = ______

4 Twenty-six first graders are going to the dairy. A bus holds fourteen students. How many buses will they need?

_____ buses

How many extra seats will there be?

_____ seats

5 seven 

s = _____ cents

1 8 + 2 + 5 + 3 = _____

2 If 25 + 34 = 59,

then _____ – 34 = _____.

3 9 – 9 = _____

8 – 8 = _____

7 – 7 = _____

6 – 6 = _____

4 Ronni rode her bike 8 blocks to Joe's house and back home. How many blocks did Ronni ride by the time she got home?

_____ blocks

5 Write a number sentence to show how many legs there are.

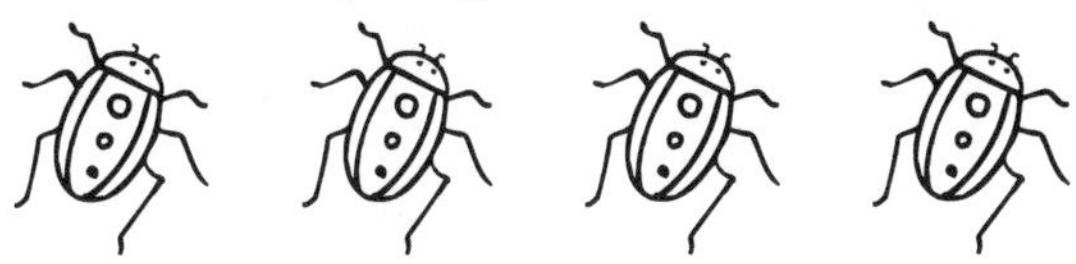

_____ + _____ + _____ + _____ = _____

1. Look at the data. Color one square on the graph for each book.

Data	
animal books	卌 |||
fairy tales	卌 ||
sports books	||
chapter books	||||
holiday books	卌

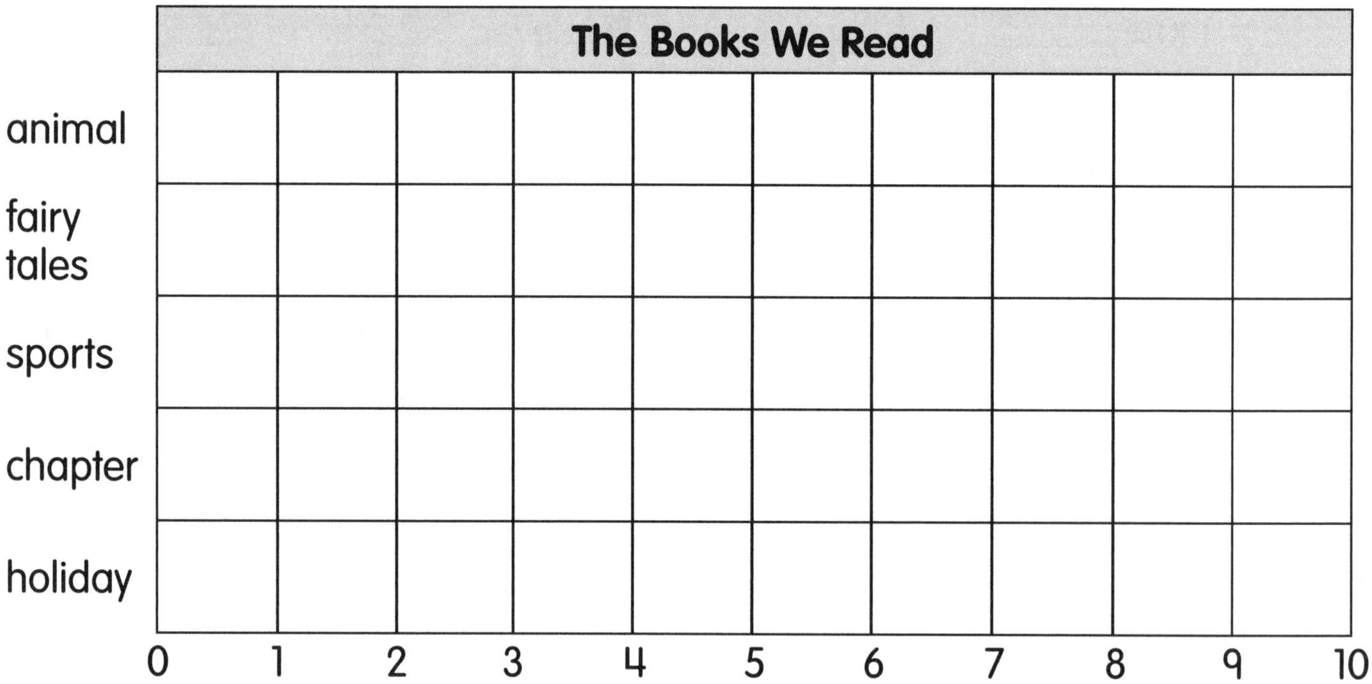

2. Look at the graph and write something you learned.

____

____

____

WEEK 35 DAY 1 Daily Math Practice

1. 4 + 5 + 3 + 0 = ____

2. Are the two parts the same?

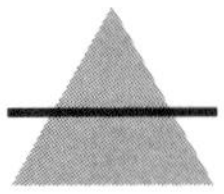

○ **yes** ○ **no**

3. If Daren pops three balloons, how many balloons will be left?

____ balloons

4. 11 + 10 = ____

12 + 10 = ____

13 + 10 = ____

14 + 10 = ____

15 + 10 = ____

5. 10 20 30 ____ ____

____ ____ ____ ____

____ ____ ____ ____

WEEK 35 DAY 2 Daily Math Practice

1. 17 – 8 = ____

2. 8 + 1 + 4 = ____

3. At the movies, 4 children are in the fourth row, 3 in the third row, 2 in the second row, and 1 in the first row. How many children are there in all?

____ children

4. If 64 – 33 = 31,

then ____ – 31 = ____.

5. Write an addition number sentence.

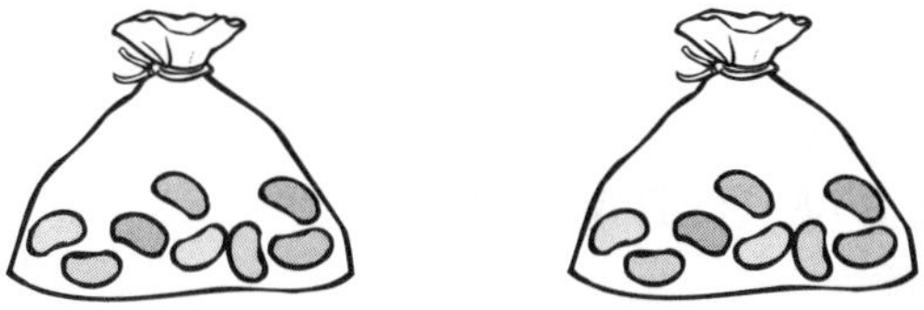

____ ◯ ____ ◯ ____

1 $5 + 2 + 7 =$ ____

2 $8 - 4 =$ ____

$38 - 34 =$ ____

3 At the game, Alec made 4 goals. He scored two points for each goal. How many points did he score in all?

____ points

4 Continue the pattern.

○ ○ □ ○ ○ □ ○

____ ____

5 About how many marshmallows?

more than 20 less than 20

1 $62 + 37 =$ ____

$37 + 62 =$ ____

2 $19 - 8 =$ ____

$19 - 9 =$ ____

3 How many sides?

one square = ____ sides

two squares = ____ sides

4 90 80 70 ____ ____ ____

____ ____ ____ ____

5 Michael is 48 inches tall. Sandi is 2 inches taller than Michael. How many inches tall is Sandi?

____ inches

Activity 1

Look at the grid. Show how to find each animal. Begin at the star.

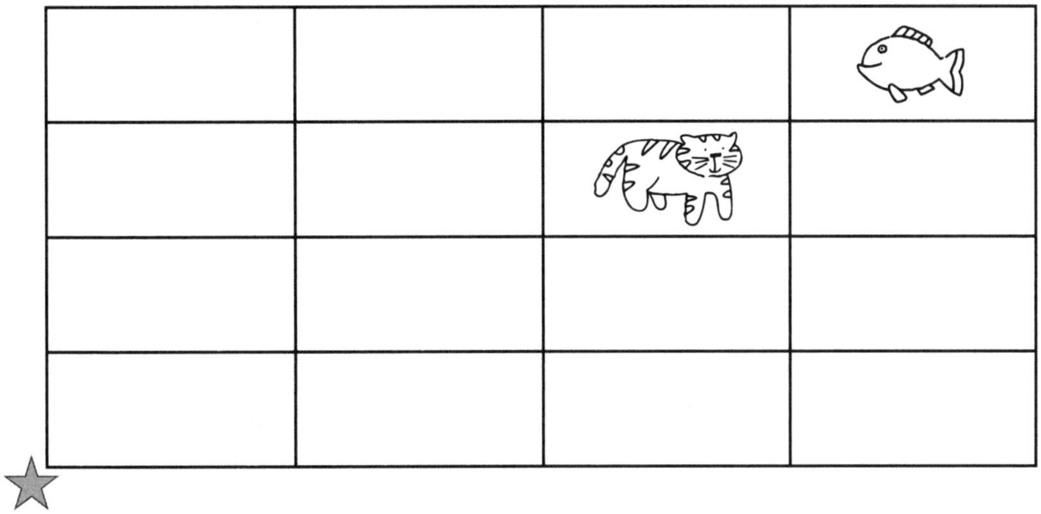

1.  over _____

up _____

2.  over _____

up _____

Activity 2

Color the numbers to count by fives.

1	2	3	4	5	6	7	8	9	10
11	12	13	14	15	16	17	18	19	20
21	22	23	24	25	26	27	28	29	30
31	32	33	34	35	36	37	38	39	40
41	42	43	44	45	46	47	48	49	50
51	52	53	54	55	56	57	58	59	60
61	62	63	64	65	66	67	68	69	70
71	72	73	74	75	76	77	78	79	80
81	82	83	84	85	86	87	88	89	90
91	92	93	94	95	96	97	98	99	100

WEEK 36 DAY 1 Daily Math Practice

1. 325 – 214 = ______

2. Color $\frac{1}{4}$.

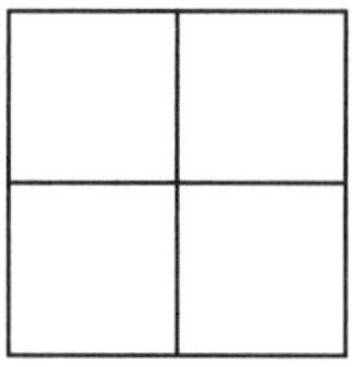

3. Sabir has two trucks, seven cars, and an ambulance. How many vehicles does he have in all?

   _____ vehicles

4. Write the correct symbol in the circle.

   < = >

   38 ◯ 46   68 ◯ 79

5. Circle the time.

   4:00

   4:30

   6:00

WEEK 36 DAY 2 Daily Math Practice

1. 47 + 22 = _____

2.

5 10 4 +10	15 +14

3. Continue the pattern.

   21 + 0   22 + 0   23 + 0

   __________   __________

4. How many?

   _____ tally marks

5. There are twenty parking spaces in the lot. Fifteen cars are parked. How many spaces are empty?

   _____ spaces

1. 89 – 34 = _____

2. 73 + 15 = _____

3. Seven friends went to the store. They each had two dollars to spend. How much money did they have altogether?

   $_________

4. Count by 2s.

   72 _____ 76 _____ 80 _____

   84 _____ 88 _____

5. Write the number.

   forty-one _____

   forty-four _____

   forty-nine _____

   fifty-two _____

1. 24 + 43 = _____

2. 38 – 6 = _____

3. Joy has seven eggs. How many more eggs does she need to fill the carton?

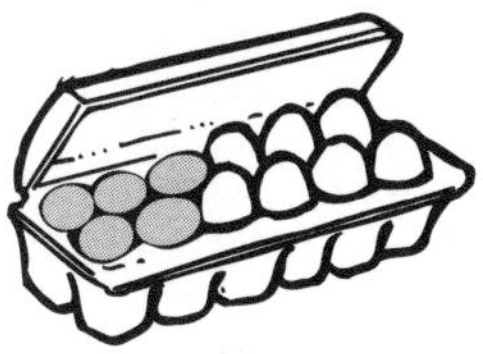

   _____ eggs

4. Continue the pattern.

   △ ▽ △ ▽ _____

   _____ _____ _____

5. Circle the clock that shows the same time.

   6:00

   12:00

   12:30

1. Josh wanted to sort his Legos®. Think about how he could sort them into two groups.

2. Draw to show which shapes would go in each group. Then write the rule.

Group 1	Group 2
This group ______________.	This group ______________.

TE = Teacher's Edition SB = Student Book

TE Page 7 / SB Page 1

WEEK 1 DAY 1 Daily Math Practice

1. 3 + 1 = 4
2. 5 + 1 = 6
3. Count up.
   1 2 3 4 5
   Count down.
   5 4 3 2 1
4. How much?
   4¢
5. Tom has one ball. He buys one more. How many does he have in all?
   + = 2 balls

WEEK 1 DAY 2 Daily Math Practice

1. 6 + 1 = 7 $\quad 6 + 1 = 7$
2. 1 + 7 = 8 $\quad 1 + 7 = 8$
3. What is one more than **two**?
   - ○ four
   - ● three
   - ○ five
4. Color the circles.
5. Write the numbers.
   1 + 2 = 3

TE Page 8 / SB Page 2

WEEK 1 DAY 3 Daily Math Practice

1. 1 + 4 = 5
2. $1 + 3 = 4 \quad 3 + 1 = 4$
3. Sam has two cats and three fish. How many pets does Sam have?
   + = ?
   5 pets
4. Add it two ways:
   + = 4
   + = 4
5. Mark the pattern unit.
   - ● AB
   - ○ ABC
   - ○ AAB

WEEK 1 DAY 4 Daily Math Practice

1. 9 + 1 = 10
   1 + 9 = 10
2. 1 + 2 = 3
3. $8 + 0 = 8 \quad 0 + 8 = 8$
4. Circle the numbers.
   4 7 a 9 2 0
   M f 3 5
5. Ann has 1 doll. Tricia has 1 doll. How many dolls are there in all?
   2 dolls

TE Page 9 / SB Page 3

WEEK 1 DAY 5 Daily Math Practice

➤ **Activity 1**

How many do you have? *Answers will vary.*

___ pockets ___ zippers ___ buttons

Check your answers with a partner.

➤ **Activity 2**

Circle the pairs. A pair = 2.

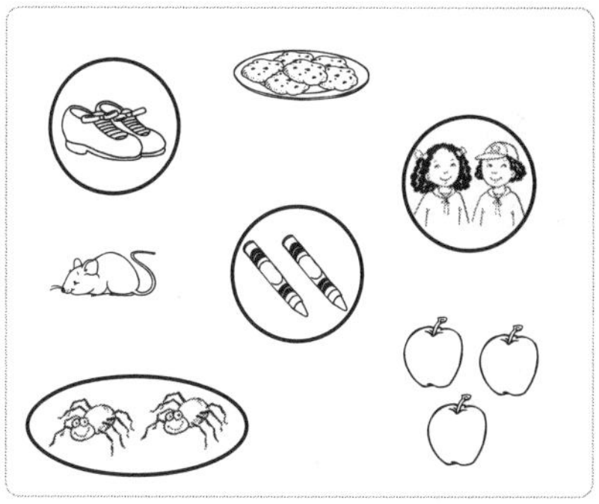

TE Page 10 / SB Page 4

WEEK 2 DAY 1 Daily Math Practice

1. Which one is heavier?
2. $1 + 2 = 3 \quad 2 + 2 = 4 \quad 3 + 2 = 5$
3. Color the second one.
   first
4. $4 + 2 = 6 \quad 2 + 4 = 6$
5. How much?
   6 cents

WEEK 2 DAY 2 Daily Math Practice

1. 6 + 2 = 8
2. 2 + 1 = 3
   1 + 2 = 3
3. The bike rack is full. It has four big bikes and two little bikes. How many bikes are there in all?
   6 bikes
4. Are there enough mittens?
   ○ yes ● no
5. Is this a triangle? △
   ● yes ○ no

TE Page 11 / SB Page 5

WEEK 2 DAY 3 Daily Math Practice

1. 2 + 7 = 9
2. 3 + 2 = 5
3. Color the ones with four wheels.
4. Write the time.
   8:00
   8 o'clock
5. Write the numbers.
   5 10 15 20 25

WEEK 2 DAY 4 Daily Math Practice

1. 8 + 2 = 10
   2 + 8 = 10
2. 5 + 2 = 7
3. Write the numbers.
   + =
   3 + 2 = 5
4. Mrs. Brown has two new pairs of shoes. How many new shoes does she have in all?
   4 shoes
5. What comes next?
   △ △ ○ △ △ ○

TE Page 12 / SB Page 6

WEEK 2 DAY 5 Daily Math Practice

Look at the graph. Then answer the questions. = **1 child**

Recess Games	
swings	4 children
balls	8 children
jump ropes	3 children
climbing bars	5 children

1. How many children played each game?
   swings 4 jump ropes 3
   balls 8 climbing bars 5
2. Which game did the most children play? balls

TE Page 13 / SB Page 7

WEEK 3 DAY 1 Daily Math Practice

1. 3 + 5 = 8
2. 4 + 3 = 7
   3 + 4 = 7
3. Write the number.
   one 1
   two 2
   three 3
4. Write = in the box if they are the same.
5. The dog had one bone. He found three more bones. How many bones did he have in all?
   4 bones

WEEK 3 DAY 2 Daily Math Practice

1. $2 + 2 = 4 \quad 3 + 3 = 6 \quad 4 + 4 = 8$
2. $7 + 3 = 10 \quad 6 + 4 = 10 \quad 5 + 5 = 10$
3. Mia had five cookies. She ate one. How many were left?
   4 cookies
4. How many?
   sides 4
   corners 4
5. Write the numbers.
   2 + 4 = 4 + 2

TE Page 14 / SB Page 8

WEEK 3 DAY 3 Daily Math Practice

1. 2 + 3 = 5
   3 + 2 = 5
2. 1 + 1 + 1 = 3
3. About how many eggs?
   2 (12) 100
4. Two birds were in the nest. One flew away. How many were left?
   1 bird
5. How many fingers?
   10
   20
   30

WEEK 3 DAY 4 Daily Math Practice

1. $3 + 8 = 11 \quad 8 + 3 = 11$
2. Write the numbers.
   + =
   3 + 3 = 6
3. Color $\frac{1}{2}$ of the ball.
4. How many?
   1 ten + 2 ones = 12
5. The train has a , a , and two . How many cars does it have in all?
   4 cars

TE Page 15 / SB Page 9

WEEK 3 DAY 5 Daily Math Practice

1. What comes next?
   □ ○ □ ○ □ ○ □ ○
   Mark the pattern unit.
   ○ ABB ● AB ○ ABCC
2. Color an AAB pattern.

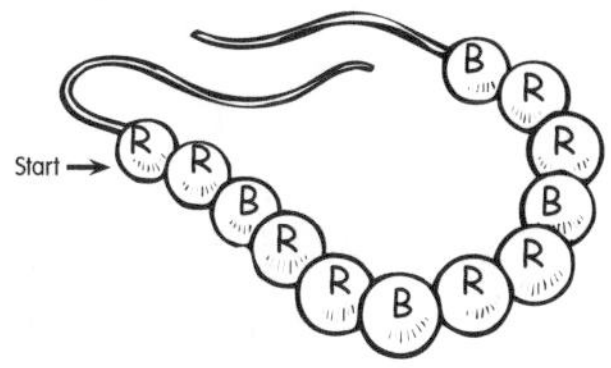

3. Draw an ABCC pattern.

   Patterns will vary, but should show an ABCC pattern.
   Sample answer:
   □ △ ○ ○ □ △ ○ ○

TE Page 16 / SB Page 10

WEEK 4 DAY 1 Daily Math Practice

1. 4 + 5 = 9
2. 2 + 4 = 6
3. What comes next? ★ ■ ▲ ★ ■ ▲
   Mark the pattern unit. ○ AB ● ABC
4. Make one tally for each flower.

1 flower	|
3 flowers	|||
4 flowers	||||

5. Mary has two birds, one turtle, and one cat. How many pets in all?
   2 + 1 + 1 = 4

WEEK 4 DAY 2 Daily Math Practice

1. 4 + 4 = 8
   5 + 5 = 10
2. 4 + 6 = 10
3. Kai has one little kitten, two little kittens, three little kittens. How many kittens does he have in all?
   6 kittens
4. Write the time.

   8 o'clock
5. Write the number.
   six 6 eight 8
   seven 7 nine 9

TE Page 17 / SB Page 11

WEEK 4 DAY 3 Daily Math Practice

1. 4 + 3 = 7
2. 4 + 7 = 11
3. Color the square blue.
   Color the circle red.
   Color the triangle yellow.
   yellow red blue
4. Bob put two cherries in the bowl.
   0 + 2 = 2
   Bob ate two cherries.
   2 − 2 = 0
5. Luis has two green hats and three red hats. How many hats does he have in all?
   5 hats

WEEK 4 DAY 4 Daily Math Practice

1. 1 + 8 = 9
2. 8 + 4 = 12; 7 + 4 = 11; 6 + 4 = 10
3. Rita has four big beads and two little beads. How many beads does she have in all?
   6 beads
4. Write the numbers.
   2 + 5 = 7
5. ○ yes ● no

TE Page 18 / SB Page 12

WEEK 4 DAY 5 Daily Math Practice

1. You will color the shapes to sort them into two groups.
   Color the shapes with 3 sides red.
   Color the shapes with 4 sides blue.

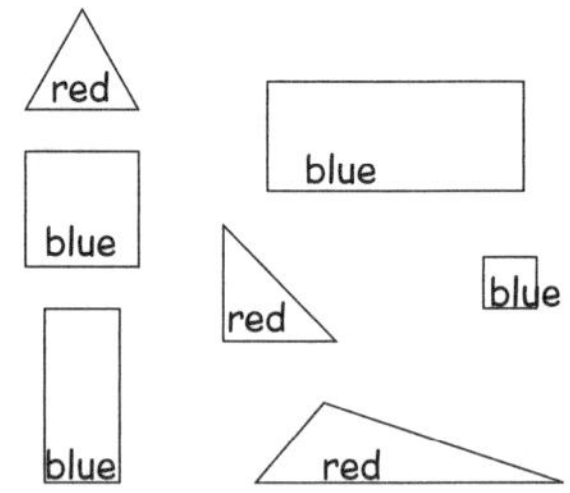

2. The red group has ____. ○ squares ● triangles
3. The blue group has squares and triangles. ○ yes ● no

TE Page 19 / SB Page 13

WEEK 5 DAY 1 Daily Math Practice

1. 5 − 1 = 4
2. 7 − 1 = 6
3. What is 3 + 3? 6
   What is 4 + 4? 8
   What is 5 + 5? 10
4. How much?

   7 cents
5. How many stamps?

   5 stamps

WEEK 5 DAY 2 Daily Math Practice

1. 2 + 4 = 6
2. 10 − 1 = 9
   1 + 9 = 10
3. Count down.
   10 9 8 7 6 5
   4 3 2 1 0
4. 3 + 2 = 5 ● yes ○ no
   2 + 3 = 5 ● yes ○ no
   5 + 2 = 3 ○ yes ● no
5. Sally ate two carrots, one apple, and four grapes. How many things did she eat?
   7 things

TE Page 20 / SB Page 14

WEEK 5 DAY 3 Daily Math Practice

1. ●●●●●●●●● ⊠
   9 − 1 = 8
2. 5 + 5 = 10 4 + 4 = 8
   3 + 3 = 6 2 + 2 = 4
3. There were ten cats in the bed and one rolled out. How many were left?
   9 cats
4. Mark the pattern unit. △△○△△○
   ○ AB ● AAB
   What shape comes next? ▲
5. Write the numbers.
   4 + 6 = 10

WEEK 5 DAY 4 Daily Math Practice

1. 10 11 12 13 14 15 16
2. 4 − 2 = 2
3. Mr. Black has five fish.
   Mr. Brown has seven fish.
   Who has more fish?
   ○ Mr. Black ● Mr. Brown
4. 6 − 1 = 5; 5 + 1 = 6
5. 4 + 0 = 4 ● yes ○ no
   0 + 4 = 4 ● yes ○ no
   4 + 4 = 0 ○ yes ● no

TE Page 21 / SB Page 15

WEEK 5 DAY 5 Daily Math Practice

1. Number the balls in order from smallest to largest.

   2 1 6 5 4 3

2. Number the dogs in order from largest to smallest.

   4 1 3 5 2

TE Page 22 / SB Page 16

WEEK 6 DAY 1 Daily Math Practice

1. 5 − 2 = 3
2. 4 + 3 = 7
   5 + 3 = 8
3. Mark has two pennies. His mom gives him three more pennies. How many pennies does he have in all?
   5 pennies
4. What time is it? 10:00
   ○ 1 o'clock
   ● 10 o'clock
   ○ 11 o'clock
5. Circle the third hat.

WEEK 6 DAY 2 Daily Math Practice

1. 8 − 2 = 6
2. 2 − 2 = 0
3. Draw a triangle. △
   How many sides? 3
   How many corners? 3
4. Which is heavier? Circle it.

5. Sean has three letters to mail. He needs a stamp for each letter. How many stamps does he need?
   3 stamps

TE Page 23 / SB Page 17

WEEK 6 DAY 3 Daily Math Practice

1. 3 4 5 6 7 8 (number line)
   7 − 2 = 5
2. 5 + 3 = 8
3. How many petals?
   5
   10
   15
   20
4. Mark the square buttons that have two holes.
   ○ ● ● ○
5. There were two red fish and five blue fish. How many fish were there in all?
   7 fish

WEEK 6 DAY 4 Daily Math Practice

1. 6 − 2 = 4
   6 − 4 = 2
2. 4 + 5 = 9
3. Ron read six pages yesterday and four pages today. How many more pages did he read yesterday?
   2 more pages
4. Mark the number sentence that tells about the picture.
   ○ 3 + 2 = 6
   ● 3 + 2 = 5
   ○ 3 − 2 = 5
5. 3 + 1 − 1 = 3

TE Page 24 / SB Page 18

WEEK 6 DAY 5 Daily Math Practice

1. Jack has 3 parrots, 2 parakeets, and 1 macaw. How many birds does he have in all?
   6 birds
   Show your work.
   3 parrots + 2 parakeets = 5; 5 + 1 macaw = 6 in all
2. If Jack can keep 2 birds in a cage, how many cages does he need?
   3 cages
   Show your work.

   2 birds + 2 birds + 2 birds = 6

TE Page 25 / SB Page 19

WEEK 7 DAY 1 Daily Math Practice

1. 5 – 3 = 2
2. 4 + 6 = 10
   3 + 6 = 9
3. There were six eggs in the box. Two eggs broke. How many are left? 4 eggs
4. Which is $\frac{1}{2}$? ○ ●
5. Write a story problem for 6 + 1 = ? Sample answer: I have 6 fish. Today I will get 1 more. How many fish will I have?

WEEK 7 DAY 2 Daily Math Practice

1. 8 – 3 = 5
2. 4 + 3 = 7
   3 + 4 = 7
3. 5 = 5 ● yes ○ no
   5 = 6 ○ yes ● no
   5 = 4 ○ yes ● no
4. What comes next?
5. There are two red beads, two blue beads, and two green beads. How many beads are there in all? 6 beads

TE Page 26 / SB Page 20

WEEK 7 DAY 3 Daily Math Practice

1. 3 – 3 = 0
2. 1 + 6 = 7
   6 + 1 = 7
3. About how many potatoes? ○ 5 ● 20 ○ 200
4. 4 + 2 = 2 + 4 ● yes ○ no
   5 + 2 = 2 + 4 ○ yes ● no
5. Write a number sentence to tell how many. 10 + 10 = 20

WEEK 7 DAY 4 Daily Math Practice

1. 9 – 3 = 6
2. 6 + 3 = 9
3. Write the number. ten 10 five 5 seven 7
4. Color the squares.
5. Tommy found three big feathers and three little feathers. How many feathers did he find in all? 6 feathers

TE Page 27 / SB Page 21

WEEK 7 DAY 5 Daily Math Practice

Mrs. Watson's class made a weather graph. Look at the graph to answer the questions.

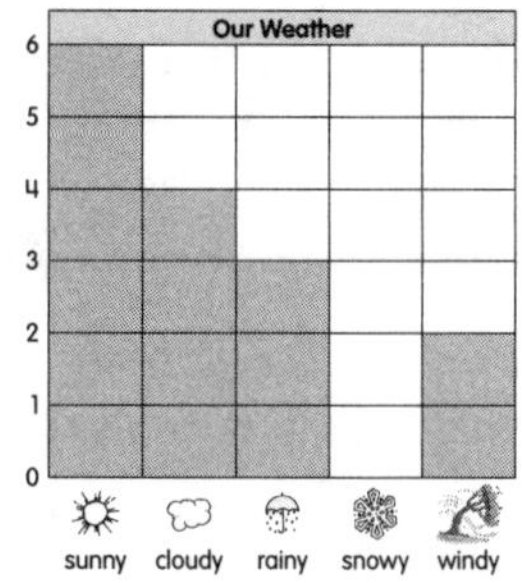

1. How many rainy days? 3
2. How many cloudy days? 4
3. Were there more rainy and cloudy days together than sunny days? ● yes ○ no
4. Write something else you know from the graph. Answers will vary. Sample answer: There were no snowy days.

TE Page 28 / SB Page 22

WEEK 8 DAY 1 Daily Math Practice

1. 3 + 7 = 10
2. 6 – 4 = 2; 2 + 4 = 6
3. Each glass holds one cup of milk. How much milk is in six glasses? 6 cups
4. ten | ones — 1 ten + 4 ones = 14
5. What comes next? ○ △ △ ○ △ △ ○

WEEK 8 DAY 2 Daily Math Practice

1. 8 – 4 = 4
2. 6 + 3 = 9; 3 + 6 = 9
3. There are five frogs on a log. If two frogs jump off, how many will be left? 3 frogs
4. What time is it? ○ 12:00 ● 9:00 ○ 9:30
5. Write the numbers. two + three + four = nine — 2 + 3 + 4 = 9

TE Page 29 / SB Page 23

WEEK 8 DAY 3 Daily Math Practice

1. 10 + 10 = 20
2. 9 – 4 = 5; 4 + 9 = 13
3. Five boys and five girls went on a hike. How many children hiked in all? 10 children
4. Count by twos. 2 4 6 8 10
5. 4 < 4 ○ yes ● no
   4 > 4 ○ yes ● no
   4 = 4 ● yes ○ no

WEEK 8 DAY 4 Daily Math Practice

1. 7 – 4 = 3
2. 10 – 5 = 5
3. There were 25 students in Mrs. White's class. Then 1 new student came. How many are in Mrs. White's class now? 26 students
4. Color the triangles.
5. Write a number sentence. 2 + 2 = 4

TE Page 30 / SB Page 24

WEEK 8 DAY 5 Daily Math Practice

➤ **Activity 1**

Count from **1** to **50**.

1	2	3	4	5	6	7	8	9	10
11	12	13	14	15	16	17	18	19	20
21	22	23	24	25	26	27	28	29	30
31	32	33	34	35	36	37	38	39	40
41	42	43	44	45	46	47	48	49	50

➤ **Activity 2**

Answer the questions.

How many ears do six elephants have? 12 ears

How many feet do four zebras have? 16 feet

How many tails do three monkeys have? 3 tails

TE Page 31 / SB Page 25

WEEK 9 DAY 1 Daily Math Practice

1. 9 – 5 = 4
2. 4 + 6 = 10
   6 + 4 = 10
3. Wes has two bags of candy. Each bag has 6 pieces. How much candy does Wes have in all? 12 pieces
4. Are the teams equal? ● yes ○ no
5. How much? 8 cents

WEEK 9 DAY 2 Daily Math Practice

1. 8 – 5 = 3
2. 4 + 5 = 9; 9 – 4 = 5
3. There are five eggs in a nest. If one egg breaks, how many will be left? 4 eggs
4. Count back. 20 19 18 17 16 15 14 13 12
5. How many tens? 3 tens

TE Page 32 / SB Page 26

WEEK 9 DAY 3 Daily Math Practice

1. 3 + 3 + 2 = 8
2. 9 – 6 = 3
   10 – 6 = 4
3. Maria's coat has 4 buttons in the front and 2 on each sleeve. How many buttons does Maria's coat have in all? 8 buttons
4. 3 + 4 = 7 ● yes ○ no
   4 – 7 = 3 ○ yes ● no
   4 + 3 = 7 ● yes ○ no
   7 – 3 = 4 ● yes ○ no
5. A square has three equal sides. ○ yes ● no
   Draw a square.

WEEK 9 DAY 4 Daily Math Practice

1. 10 – 4 = 6
2. 7 + 2 = 9
   9 – 7 = 2
3. Josh has three beanbags, and Todd has four. Who has more? Todd How many more? 1
4. Mark the pattern unit. ○ AB ○ AAB ● ABB
5. What comes next? 19 20 21 22
   47 48 49 50

TE Page 33 / SB Page 27

WEEK 9 DAY 5 Daily Math Practice

➤ **Activity 1**

Write your name in two different patterns.

Examples:

Pattern: PEtePEtePEte PeTePeTePeTe

Pattern Unit: AABB AB

Patterns will vary, but should match the pattern unit name.

Name the pattern unit. ______

Name the pattern unit. ______

➤ **Activity 2**

Write the missing numbers.

10 20 30 40 50 60 70 80 90 100 110

5 10 15 20 25 30 35 40 45 50 55

2 4 6 8 10 12 14 16 18 20 22 24

TE Page 34 / SB Page 28

WEEK 10 DAY 1 Daily Math Practice

1. 12 − 2 = 10
2. 5 + 3 + 1 = 9; 5 + 4 = 9
3. The apple tree had six apples. Bob picked two. How many apples were left? 4 apples
4. Color the fifth duck.
5. 4 + 2 = 6 ● yes ○ no
   3 + 3 = 6 ● yes ○ no
   6 + 0 = 6 ● yes ○ no
   5 + 2 = 6 ○ yes ● no

WEEK 10 DAY 2 Daily Math Practice

1. 10 − 7 = 3
   11 − 7 = 4
2. 8 + 3 = 11
3. Jenny picked up two pennies. She put them with her other six pennies. How many pennies does Jenny have now? 8 pennies
4. Circle the hats that have stripes and bills.
5. Write the time. 6:00 — 6 o'clock

TE Page 35 / SB Page 29

WEEK 10 DAY 3 Daily Math Practice

1. 5 + 2 + 4 = 11
2. What number is one less? 12 13; 25 26
3. Sue had a double scoop of ice cream. Tom had a triple scoop. Who had the smallest amount? ● Sue ○ Tom
4. How many? 2; 4; 6; 8
5. Which weighs more? ○ (one banana) ● (bunch of bananas)

WEEK 10 DAY 4 Daily Math Practice

1. 9 − 8 = 1
   12 − 11 = 1
2. 9 + 7 = 16
3. Tommy had 10 cents. He bought a pencil for 5 cents. How much does he have left? 5 cents
4. Color the squares.
5. Four cherries and five grapes equal 9 pieces of fruit.

TE Page 36 / SB Page 30

WEEK 10 DAY 5 Daily Math Practice

Activity 1

Use the number line to solve the problem.

1 2 3 4 5 6 7 8 9 10 11 12 13 14

10 − 5 + 6 − 1 + 4 − 2 = 12

Show your work here.

10 − 5 = 5; 5 + 6 = 11; 11 − 1 = 10; 10 + 4 = 14; 14 − 2 = 12

Activity 2

Count from **51** to **110**.

51	52	53	54	55	56	57	58	59	60
61	62	63	64	65	66	67	68	69	70
71	72	73	74	75	76	77	78	79	80
81	82	83	84	85	86	87	88	89	90
91	92	93	94	95	96	97	98	99	100
101	102	103	104	105	106	107	108	109	110

TE Page 37 / SB Page 31

WEEK 11 DAY 1 Daily Math Practice

1. 5 + 5 = 10
   5 + 4 = 9
2. 12 − 2 = 10
3. Juan's family ate four tortillas for lunch and four tortillas for dinner. How many did they eat in all? 8 tortillas
4. Write the number.
   eight 8
   four 4
   twelve 12
   zero 0
5. 2 + 2 + 2 + 2 = 8
   10 + 10 + 10 + 10 = 40

WEEK 11 DAY 2 Daily Math Practice

1. 8 + 3 = 11
   11 − 8 = 3
2. 3 + 2 + 3 = 8
3. I saw six sea stars, three snails, and a sunfish at the beach. How many animals did I see? 10 animals
4. Color $\frac{1}{2}$. Color 1 whole.
5. 5 + 4 = 4 + 5 ● yes ○ no
   6 + 4 = 4 + 5 ○ yes ● no

TE Page 38 / SB Page 32

WEEK 11 DAY 3 Daily Math Practice

1. 10 + 9 = 19
   19 − 10 = 9
2. 2 + 6 = 8
3. 10 = 5 + 4 ○ yes ● no
   10 < 5 + 4 ○ yes ● no
   10 > 5 + 4 ● yes ○ no
4. Draw three circles. Color one blue. Color two red.
   blue red red
   Write a number sentence to tell about the circles.
   1 + 2 = 3
5. 5 boys + 5 girls + 1 dog = 11

WEEK 11 DAY 4 Daily Math Practice

1. 44 45 46 47 48 49
   45 + 3 = 48
2. 11 12 13 14 15 16 17 18
   17 − 5 = 12
3. Three girls each have three bears. How many bears do they have in all? 9 bears
4. About how many crayons? ○ almost 6 ● almost 20 ○ almost 160
5. Write four number sentences using **4**, **2**, and **6**.
   4 + 2 = 6
   2 + 4 = 6
   6 − 2 = 4
   6 − 4 = 2

TE Page 39 / SB Page 33

WEEK 11 DAY 5 Daily Math Practice

For nine months, the students in Mrs. Timm's class put a (tooth) on a graph every time one of them lost a tooth. Look at the graph to answer the questions.

Teeth Lost	(tooth) = 1 tooth
September	3
October	5
November	2
December	4
January	3
February	
March	1
April	2
May	3

1. How many teeth have been lost in all? 23 teeth
2. In which month were the most teeth lost? ○ February ● October ○ May
3. In which month were the fewest teeth lost? ○ March ○ September ● February

TE Page 40 / SB Page 34

WEEK 12 DAY 1 Daily Math Practice

1. 4 + 3 = 7; 14 + 3 = 17
2. 7 − 4 = 3; 7 − 3 = 4
3. Mr. Smith sold two bags of oranges. If each bag has eight oranges, how many oranges did he sell in all? 16 oranges
4. Write the time. 11 o'clock
5. Draw tally marks to show how many.
   6 — 卌 |
   3 — |||
   5 — 卌

WEEK 12 DAY 2 Daily Math Practice

1. 6 + 6 = 12
   6 + 6 + 6 = 18
2. 30 + 20 = 50
3. There are two raisins on each cookie. How many raisins are there on three cookies? 6 raisins
4. Continue the pattern.
   2 2 1 2 2 1 2 2 1 2 2 1
5. Count the eyes. 2 4 6 8

TE Page 41 / SB Page 35

WEEK 12 DAY 3 Daily Math Practice

1. How many? 15
2. 54 + 1 = 55
3. There are two peanuts in each shell. How many peanuts are in six shells? 12 peanuts
4. Draw an **X** on the spheres.
5. Add two. 5 + 2 = 7
   Then subtract two. 7 − 2 = 5

WEEK 12 DAY 4 Daily Math Practice

1. 4 + 3 + 2 + 1 = 10
2. 13 − 7 = 6
   7 + 6 = 13
3. Jose read two books every day. How many books did he read in five days? 10 books
4. Write the number.
   thirty-six 36
   twenty-seven 27
5. Draw an **X** on $\frac{1}{4}$.

TE Page 42 / SB Page 36

WEEK 12 DAY 5 Daily Math Practice

Sienna went to the store to buy snacks. She bought four muffins, six oranges, and five carrots. Draw the snacks on the chart.

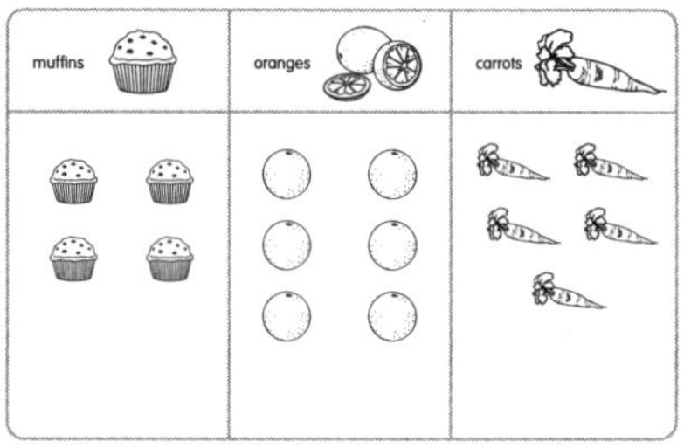

Use the chart to answer the questions.

1. How many snacks did Sienna buy in all?
   4 + 6 + 5 = 15 snacks
2. Sienna ate one muffin. How many snacks does she have now?
   15 − 1 = 14 snacks left

TE Page 43 / SB Page 37

WEEK 13 DAY 1 Daily Math Practice

1. How many? (16 dots) = 16
2. 20 – 10 = 10
3. Carl rode his bike two blocks to the park and two blocks home. How far did he ride? 4 blocks
4. Which pattern is shown below? ○ ABA ● AABB ○ ABBA
5. How much? 40 cents

WEEK 13 DAY 2 Daily Math Practice

1. 0 + 15 = 7 + 8 ● yes ○ no
2. 2 + 9 = 11
3. 3 + 4 = 7; 7 – 3 = 4
4. Draw an **X** on the circles.
5. Brett and Bonnie ate pizza for lunch. They each had four pieces. How many pieces did they eat in all? 8 pieces

TE Page 44 / SB Page 38

WEEK 13 DAY 3 Daily Math Practice

1. 6 + 4 = 10; 7 + 3 = 10
2. 14 – 13 = 1
3. 1 + 15 = 16 ● yes ○ no; 15 + 1 = 16 ● yes ○ no; 16 + 1 = 15 ○ yes ● no
4. Write a story problem about birds for **5 – 2 = 3**. Sample answer: Five birds were sitting in a tree. Then two flew away. How many birds were left?
5. How much? = 10 ¢

WEEK 13 DAY 4 Daily Math Practice

1. 6 + 4 < 7 + 7 ● yes ○ no
2. 14 – 2 = 12
3. Seline put three cookies and two brownies in a box for her grandma. How many treats will her grandma have altogether? 5 treats
4. Circle **odd** or **even**. odd (even); (odd) even; odd (even)
5. Circle the ways to make **7**. (5 + 2) 4 + 4 (6 + 1) (9 – 2) 3 + 5 (7 + 0)

TE Page 45 / SB Page 39

WEEK 13 DAY 5 Daily Math Practice

1. Mark has to buy two new tires for his bike. If each tire costs $10.00, how much money does Mark need? $ 20.00

2. Mark has $15.00 in his bank, and he got $5.00 for doing jobs. Can he buy the tires? ● yes ○ no

Explain: $15.00 + $5.00 = $20.00 Mark has $20.00. The tires cost $20.00, so he can buy them.

TE Page 46 / SB Page 40

WEEK 14 DAY 1 Daily Math Practice

1. 3 + 9 = 12; 9 + 3 = 12
2. 15 + 1 = 16; 16 – 1 = 15
3. Sammy found two nickels in his pocket. How much did he find? 10 ¢
4. Draw an **X** on the seventh bird.
5. 5 10 15 20 25 30 35 40 45 50 55 60 65 70

WEEK 14 DAY 2 Daily Math Practice

1. 2 + 9 = 11; 2 + 10 = 12; 2 + 11 = 13
2. 11 – 5 = 6; 11 – 6 = 5
3. Which is heavier? 10 pounds (100 pounds)
4. Write the time. 9:00 9 o'clock
5. There were six flowers in the vase. Two of the flowers were roses. How many flowers were **not** roses? 4 flowers

TE Page 47 / SB Page 41

WEEK 14 DAY 3 Daily Math Practice

1. 5 + 6 = 11; 6 + 5 = 11
2. 16 – 8 = 8; 8 + 8 = 16
3. Trina saw three pigs, two cows, and four chickens on the farm. How many animals did she see in all? 9 animals
4. Draw a rectangle. Write how many. 4 sides 4 corners
5. 12 = 4 + 8 ● yes ○ no; 8 = 12 + 4 ○ yes ● no; 12 = 8 + 4 ● yes ○ no

WEEK 14 DAY 4 Daily Math Practice

1. 7 – 5 = 2; 8 – 5 = 3
2. 4 + 8 = 12
3. Five pairs of ants marched up the hill. How many ants were there in all? 10 ants
4. Circle the ways to make **nine**. (3 + 6) (4 + 5) (2 + 7) 1 + 7 (0 + 9) 4 + 4
5. How much? 31 cents

TE Page 48 / SB Page 42

WEEK 14 DAY 5 Daily Math Practice

1. How many toes?

1 baby	10 toes
2 babies	20 toes
3 babies	30 toes

How many toes do 5 babies have? 50 toes

2. How many ears?

3 rabbits	6 ears
4 rabbits	8 ears
5 rabbits	10 ears

How many ears do 6 rabbits have? 12 ears

TE Page 49 / SB Page 43

WEEK 15 DAY 1 Daily Math Practice

1. 5 + 7 = 11 + 0 ○ yes ● no
2. 10 – 3 = 7; 20 – 3 = 17
3. There were two goldfish and four red fish in the bowl. How many fish were there in all? 6 fish
4. Are the two sides the same? ● yes ○ no; ○ yes ● no
5. Finish the pattern.

WEEK 15 DAY 2 Daily Math Practice

1. 5 + 8 = 13; 8 + 5 = 13
2. 4 – 4 = 0; 25 – 25 = 0
3. The bag had ten cookies in it. If Eli ate two and Molly ate one, how many cookies were left? 7 cookies
4. Mark the pizza divided in half. ● ○
5. Write the number. eleven 11; thirteen 13; fourteen 14

TE Page 50 / SB Page 44

WEEK 15 DAY 3 Daily Math Practice

1. 7 + 5 = 12; 12 – 7 = 5
2. 4 + 2 + 1 = 7
3. 9 < 3 ○ yes ● no; 19 > 13 ● yes ○ no
4. About how many paper clips? ○ 5 ○ 15 ● 50
5. Bingo hid four bones in the garden and two bones in the park. How many bones did he hide in all? 6 bones

WEEK 15 DAY 4 Daily Math Practice

1. 4 + 9 = 13; 5 + 8 = 13; 6 + 7 = 13
2. 18 – 1 = 17 + 0 ● yes ○ no
3. Four trucks and six cars were stopped at a light. How many vehicles were stopped in all? 10 vehicles
4. Write four number sentences using **3**, **5**, and **8**. 3 + 5 = 8; 5 + 3 = 8; 8 – 3 = 5; 8 – 5 = 3
5. Are both sides the same? ○ yes ● no

TE Page 51 / SB Page 45

WEEK 15 DAY 5 Daily Math Practice

Activity 1 (cake) = 1 birthday

March

Sun.	Mon.	Tues.	Wed.	Thurs.	Fri.	Sat.
			1	2	3	4 (birthday)
5	6	7 (birthday)	8	9	10	11
12	13	14 (birthday)	15	16	17 (birthday)	18
19	20	21	22	23	24	25
26	27	28 (birthday)	29	30	31	

1. How many birthdays are there in March? 5 birthdays
2. What day of the week has the most birthdays? ○ Sunday ● Tuesday ○ Friday
3. There is only one birthday on the weekend. ● yes ○ no

Activity 2

Use this number line to mark **yes** or **no** for each number sentence.

1 2 3 4 5 6 7 8 9 10 11 12 13 14

1. 10 > 11 ○ yes ● no
2. 14 = 13 + 1 ● yes ○ no
3. 12 < 9 ○ yes ● no
4. 7 > 3 ● yes ○ no

TE Page 52 / SB Page 46

WEEK 16 DAY 1 Daily Math Practice

1. 6 + 8 = 14
   8 + 6 = 14
2. 15 − 7 = 8
   8 + 7 = 15
3. What comes next?
   2 4 6 8 10 12 14 16
4. Which shows $\frac{1}{4}$?
   ○ (circle in halves) ● (circle in quarters)
5. Keli is 11. Her sister is 6. How many years older than her sister is Keli?
   5 years older

WEEK 16 DAY 2 Daily Math Practice

1. 7 + 7 = 14
   7 − 7 = 0
2. 10 + 10 + 10 = 30
3. Tony swam four laps of freestyle and six laps of backstroke. How many laps did he swim in all?
   10 laps
4. Continue the pattern.
   □△○□△○
   □ △ ○
5. How many?
   𝍸𝍸 𝍸𝍸 ||
   ○ 11 ● 12 ○ 21

TE Page 53 / SB Page 47

WEEK 16 DAY 3 Daily Math Practice

1. 7 − 6 = 1 + 0
   ● yes ○ no
2. 9 + 3 = 12
   9 + 4 = 13
3. I have seven sharp pencils and two broken pencils. How many pencils do I have in all?
   9 pencils
4. If 53 + 4 = 57, then 57 − 4 = 53
5. Write the number.
   four 4
   twenty-one 21
   thirty 30
   thirty-two 32

WEEK 16 DAY 4 Daily Math Practice

1. 6 + 10 = 16
   6 + 9 = 15
2. 10 − 2 = 7 − 0
   ○ yes ● no
3. Jamal hit three balls. Ann hit four balls. Terri didn't get a hit. How many hits were there in all?
   7 hits
4. What time is it?

   10 o'clock
5. Color the bigger square.
   ▭ □ △ ■

TE Page 54 / SB Page 48

WEEK 16 DAY 5 Daily Math Practice

On Monday, four girls checked out 3 books each.
On Tuesday, two of the girls returned their books.

1. How many books are still checked out? 6 books

   Show your work here.

2. Each girl reads 3 books every day. How many books will each girl read in 3 days?
   9 books

TE Page 55 / SB Page 49

WEEK 17 DAY 1 Daily Math Practice

1. 7 + 8 = 15   15 − 7 = 8
2. 9 + 2 = 11 + 0
   ● yes ○ no
3. Two polar bears were walking across the ice. Six more polar bears joined them. How many were there in all?
   8 polar bears
4. 35 34 33 32 31 30 29 28 27
5. Write four number sentences using **6**, **5**, and **11**.
   6 + 5 = 11
   5 + 6 = 11
   11 − 6 = 5
   11 − 5 = 6

WEEK 17 DAY 2 Daily Math Practice

1. 15 − 7 = 8   15 − 8 = 7
2. 9 + 5 = 14
   7 + 7 = 14
3. Each drummer needs two drumsticks. How many drumsticks do five drummers need?
   10 drumsticks
4. 3 + 3 + 3 = 9
   4 + 4 + 4 = 12
5. Write an addition story to tell about the fish. Sample answer:

   I saw two big fish and five little fish in the lake. How many fish did I see in all?

TE Page 56 / SB Page 50

WEEK 17 DAY 3 Daily Math Practice

1. 9 + 7 = 16
2. 9 − 2 = 7
   2 + 7 = 9
3. Juanita had three cupcakes. She gave one to Felix and two to the twins. How many cupcakes did she have left?
   0 cupcakes
4. 10 20 30 40 50 60 70 80 90 100
5. How many sides?
   △ 3
   ▭ 4
   ⬠ 5

WEEK 17 DAY 4 Daily Math Practice

1. 8 + 5 = 13
2. 20 − 10 = 10
3. The hungry caterpillar ate three leaves, two strawberries, and five grapes. How many things did it eat in all?
   10 things
4. Write the rule for each group. Sample answers:
   Group 1: Group 1 has flowers with 4 petals.
   Group 2: Group 2 has flowers with 5 petals.
5. If 34 + 7 = 41, then
   41 − 7 = 34.

TE Page 57 / SB Page 51

WEEK 17 DAY 5 Daily Math Practice

1. Measure the **longest** side of a book with your pencil.
   My book is ____ pencils long. Answers will vary, but should accurately reflect lengths measured with students' pencils.
2. Look at the picture to answer the questions.

   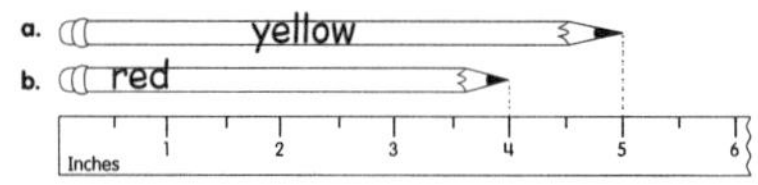

   Color the longer pencil yellow.
   Color the shorter pencil red.
   How long is each pencil? a. 5 inches b. 4 inches
   How much longer is the yellow pencil than the red pencil?
   1 inch longer
3. Add or subtract.

2 inches	5 inches	3 inches
+ 3 inches	− 1 inch	+ 3 inches
5 inches	4 inches	6 inches

TE Page 58 / SB Page 52

WEEK 18 DAY 1 Daily Math Practice

1. 7 + 9 = 16
   7 + 11 = 18
2. 15 − 9 = 6
   15 − 6 = 9
3. Which is heavier? Circle it.
   2 grams (51 pounds)
   (20 grams) 15 pounds
4. Draw an **X** on the eighth bead.
   first →
   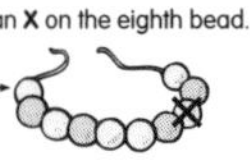
5. Lilly drew five hearts. She colored two of them red. She colored the rest pink. How many hearts are pink?
   3 pink hearts

WEEK 18 DAY 2 Daily Math Practice

1. 10 + 0 = 10   10 + 5 = 15   10 + 10 = 20
2. If 17 − 5 = 12, then 12 + 5 = 17
3. Circle the one that does **not** belong.

4. What time is it?
   4:00   4 o'clock
5. Mike invited seven friends to his party. Two cannot come. How many friends will be there?
   5 friends

TE Page 59 / SB Page 53

WEEK 18 DAY 3 Daily Math Practice

1. 9 + 8 = 17
   17 − 9 = 8
2. 5 + 10 = 15
   15 − 5 = 10
3. Count by 5s.
   50 55 60 65 70 75 80
4. 7 tens + 6 ones = 76
   5 tens + 0 ones = 50
5. David bought two apples for $1.00. How much would four apples cost?
   $2.00

WEEK 18 DAY 4 Daily Math Practice

1. 5 + 10 = 15
   5 + 9 = 14
2. 8 − 7 = 1
   15 − 14 = 1
3. Circle the ways to make **eleven**.
   (10 + 1) 12 − 2 (5 + 6)
   (11 + 0) (15 − 4) 9 + 1
4. A square has 4 sides.
   A triangle has 3 sides.
5. Four bees flew to three flowers. How many more bees are there than flowers?
   1 more bee

TE Page 60 / SB Page 54

WEEK 18 DAY 5 Daily Math Practice

1. How many squares in all? 10 squares

   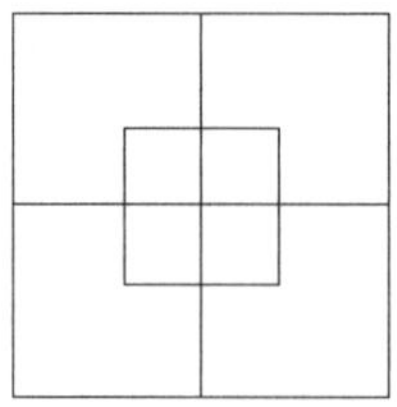

2. How many squares in all? 14 squares

   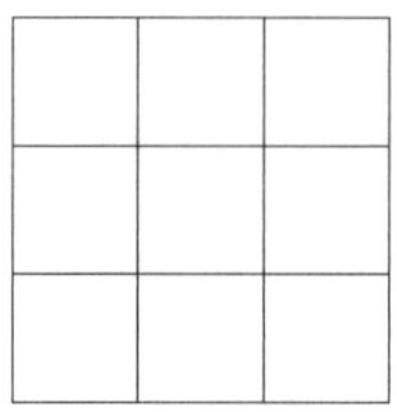

TE Page 61 / SB Page 55

WEEK 19 DAY 1 Daily Math Practice

1. 8 + 8 = 16
   9 + 9 = 18
2. 6 − 3 = 3
   8 − 4 = 4
3. Six girls formed two equal teams. How many girls were on each team?
   3 girls
4. If 36 + 42 = 78, then
   42 + 36 = 78.
5. Color $\frac{1}{2}$ of the rectangle.
   $\frac{1}{2}$ < 1 whole
   ● yes ○ no

WEEK 19 DAY 2 Daily Math Practice

1. 5 + 5 = 10
   6 + 5 = 11
2. 12 − 2 = 10
3. Carrie planted three rows of tulips. She put six bulbs in each row. How many bulbs did she plant in all?
   18 bulbs
4. Write a subtraction story for the picture.

   Sample answer:
   There were 8 worms.
   A bird ate 1. How many
   worms were left?
5. What is 10 more than 20? 30

TE Page 62 / SB Page 56

WEEK 19 DAY 3 Daily Math Practice

1. 13 − 9 = 4
2. How many in all?
   ●●●●● ●●●●● = 10
3. Kendra needs four chairs. She borrowed two from Gavin and two from Tami. How many more chairs does she need?
   0 more chairs
4. 14 = 15 ○ yes ● no
   14 < 15 ● yes ○ no
   14 > 15 ○ yes ● no
5. About how many pounds of potatoes?
   1 pound
   (10 pounds)
   100 pounds

WEEK 19 DAY 4 Daily Math Practice

1. 8 − 1 = 10 − 1
   ○ yes ● no
2. 10 − 5 = 5
   20 − 5 = 15
3. Color the squares red.
   Color the rectangles yellow.
   red yellow red yellow
4. Are both sides the same?
   ● yes ○ no
5. Brad checked out five books and James checked out three books. How many books did they check out altogether?
   8 books

TE Page 63 / SB Page 57

WEEK 19 DAY 5 Daily Math Practice

Look at the graph to answer the questions.

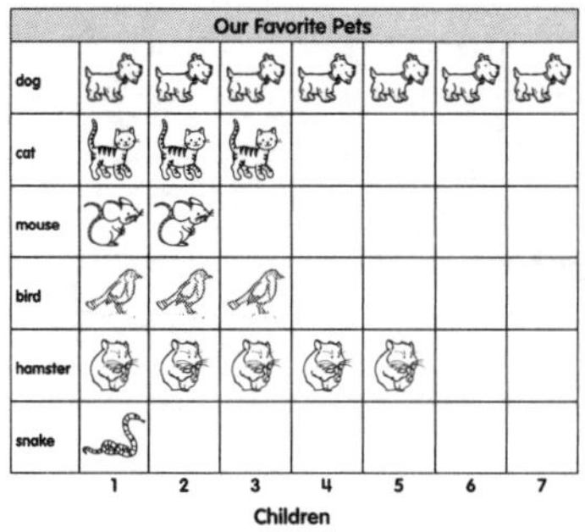

1. Which pet is the most favorite? dog
2. Which pet is the least favorite? snake
3. Which **two** pets were picked by the same number of children?
   cat and bird
4. Write something else you learned from the graph. Answers will vary. Sample answer:
   More children like hamsters than cats.

TE Page 64 / SB Page 58

WEEK 20 DAY 1 Daily Math Practice

1. 13 − 2 = 11
   2 + 11 = 13
2. 6 + 10 = 16
   7 + 10 = 17
3. Bea made ten cookies. She put three candies on each cookie. How many candies did she use?
   30 candies
4. Color $\frac{1}{4}$.
5. Write the numbers.
   eleven 11
   seventeen 17
   thirty-eight 38

WEEK 20 DAY 2 Daily Math Practice

1. 4 + 8 = 12
   12 − 8 = 4
2. 15 − 4 = 11
3. Continue the pattern.
4. How many?
   14 tally marks
5. The bus had fifteen passengers. Four got off at the first stop. Two got off at the second stop. How many passengers were left?
   9 passengers

TE Page 65 / SB Page 59

WEEK 20 DAY 3 Daily Math Practice

1. 2 + 9 = 11 + 0
   ● yes ○ no
2. 8 − 6 = 2 18 − 6 = 12
3. Bob piled blocks in stacks of five. He made six stacks. How many blocks did he use in all?
   30 blocks
4. 2 4 6 8 10 12 14 16 18 20
5. Color the cones.

WEEK 20 DAY 4 Daily Math Practice

1. 100 + 4 = 104
2. 5 + 1 + 2 = 8 5 + 3 = 8
3. Ten balls were in the box. The first graders are using seven of them. How many balls are left?
   3 balls
4. Write the time.
   3 o'clock
5. If 20 + 30 = 50,
   then 50 − 30 = 20.

TE Page 66 / SB Page 60

WEEK 20 DAY 5 Daily Math Practice

1. Doug went fishing. He had 12 worms in a can and 3 in his pocket.
   Draw Doug's worms.

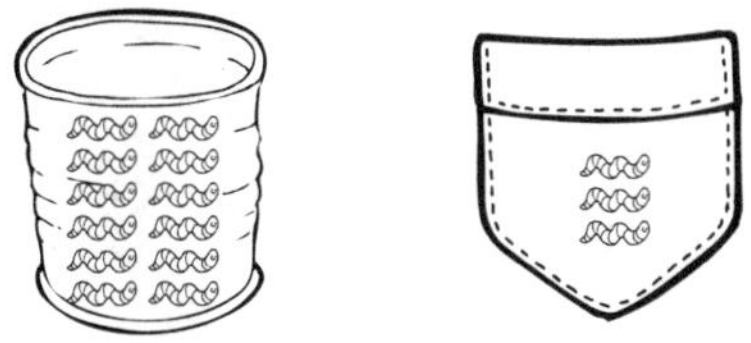

2. Doug put a new worm on the hook after every fish he got. He has four worms left. How many fish did he get?
   11 fish

   Show your work here.

   12 worms
   + 3 worms
   15 worms

   15
   − 4 worms left
   11 fish caught

TE Page 67 / SB Page 61

WEEK 21 DAY 1 Daily Math Practice

1. 7 + 10 = 17
   17 + 10 = 27
2. 6 − 5 = 16 − 15 ● yes ○ no
3. Rick has two bags of cans to recycle. Joe has three bags. How many bags do they have in all?
   5 bags
4. Draw an **X** on the closed figures.
5. Write four number sentences using **6**, **2**, and **8**.
   6 + 2 = 8
   2 + 6 = 8
   8 − 6 = 2
   8 − 2 = 6

WEEK 21 DAY 2 Daily Math Practice

1. 6 + 7 = 13
   7 + 6 = 13
2. 3 + 8 + 2 = 13
3. 1 ten = 10 4 tens = 40
   2 tens = 20 5 tens = 50
   3 tens = 30 6 tens = 60
4. Mark the pattern unit.
   ○ AB ○ ABB ● AABB
5. Bill walked four blocks to Sam's house, and then he walked back home. How many blocks did he walk in all?
   8 blocks

TE Page 68 / SB Page 62

WEEK 21 DAY 3 Daily Math Practice

1. 647 + 0 = 647
   647 + 1 = 648
2. 8 + 6 = 14
   18 + 6 = 24
3. Which stem is longer?
4. If 7 + 3 = 10, then
   10 − 3 = 7.
5. Tom put three balls, one jump rope, and four beanbags into the bin. How many toys did Tom put into the bin in all?
   8 toys

WEEK 21 DAY 4 Daily Math Practice

1. 8 + 9 = 17
2. 10 − 6 = 4
3. How much?
   30 cents
4. **Five** is an odd number.
   ● yes ○ no
5. Terri and her sister have two bikes and a wagon. How many wheels are there altogether?
   8 wheels

TE Page 69 / SB Page 63

WEEK 21 DAY 5 Daily Math Practice

1. The cook needs one cup of cheese for each pizza. Each package of cheese holds four cups. The class ordered eight pizzas. How many packages of cheese will the cook need?
   2 packages

   Show your work here.
   Cheese Cheese
   The cook will need
   2 packages of cheese.

2. Mark the pizza that shows fourths.

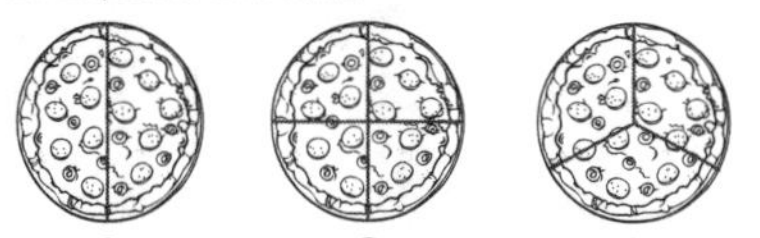

   ○ ● ○

TE Page 70 / SB Page 64

WEEK 22 DAY 1 Daily Math Practice

1. 50 + 10 = 60
2. 10 + 1 = 11; 10 + 2 = 12; 10 + 3 = 13
3. Draw an **X** on the heaviest.
4. Write the time. 2:00 — 2 o'clock
5. The ball box has two basketballs, three tennis balls, five soccer balls, and one baseball. How many balls are there in all? 11 balls

WEEK 22 DAY 2 Daily Math Practice

1. 9 + 3 = 12; 12 − 9 = 3
2. 23 − 1 = 22; 47 − 1 = 46
3. If 6 + 7 = 13, then 13 − 7 = 6.
4. Write 5 more. 20 25; 40 45; 30 35; 50 55
5. Five days in every week are school days. How many days are **not** school days? 2 days

TE Page 71 / SB Page 65

WEEK 22 DAY 3 Daily Math Practice

1. 1 ten + 6 ones = 16
2. 17 − 7 = 10; 7 + 10 = 17
3. Chuck planted four trees. One tree died, so he planted another one. How many trees did he plant in all? 5 trees
4. How much? 25 cents
5. Circle the ways to make **8**. (5 + 3) 2 + 7 (4 + 4) 6 + 1 (8 + 0) 16 − 7

WEEK 22 DAY 4 Daily Math Practice

1. 4 + 7 + 3 = 14
2. 10 − 0 = 10; 10 − 3 = 7; 10 − 1 = 9; 10 − 4 = 6; 10 − 2 = 8; 10 − 5 = 5
3. The fourth mitten has stripes. ● yes ○ no
4. Circle the straight lines.
5. Cam and Jack took five boxes to the recycling center. The man paid them $1.00. If they share the money equally, how much will each boy get? 50¢

TE Page 72 / SB Page 66

WEEK 22 DAY 5 Daily Math Practice

➤ Activity 1

1. Mark the name of the solid figure. ● cube ○ sphere ○ square
2. How many sides? 6
3. Can it stack? ● yes ○ no
4. Can it roll? ○ yes ● no

➤ Activity 2

Tess built this stack of cubes.

Which drawing shows how the stack looks from the shaded side?

TE Page 73 / SB Page 67

WEEK 23 DAY 1 Daily Math Practice

1. 10 + 8 = 18; 12 + 8 = 20
2. 8 − 0 = 8; 18 − 8 = 10
3. Three birds each laid three eggs. How many eggs are there in all? 9 eggs
4. Color $\frac{1}{2}$ of all the pigs.
5. Write the number. zero 0; eight 8; twenty-four 24; forty-two 42

WEEK 23 DAY 2 Daily Math Practice

1. 6 + 7 = 13; 7 + 6 = 13
2. 2 tens + 3 ones = 23
3. Are both sides the same? ● yes ○ no
4. Circle the time. 6:30 7:30 (8:30)
5. Pam gives her dog a bone every morning and every night. How many bones does she give her dog in one week? 14 bones

TE Page 74 / SB Page 68

WEEK 23 DAY 3 Daily Math Practice

1. 9 + 7 = 16
2. How many in all? = 15
3. Continue the pattern.
4. Color the rectangles.
5. The nurse saw 4 boys and 6 girls with colds. How many children did she see in all? 10 children

WEEK 23 DAY 4 Daily Math Practice

1. 15 − 6 = 9; 6 + 9 = 15
2. 2 + 7 + 4 = 13
3. Angela has four pink jelly beans and five purple jelly beans. If she eats three jelly beans, how many will she have left? 6 jelly beans
4. 9 + 10 = 19; 10 + 10 = 20
5. Write four number sentences using **2**, **7**, and **9**. 2 + 7 = 9; 7 + 2 = 9; 9 − 2 = 7; 9 − 7 = 2

TE Page 75 / SB Page 69

WEEK 23 DAY 5 Daily Math Practice

Circle **yes** if both sides are the same.
Circle **no** if both sides are **not** the same.

1. ● yes ○ no | ○ yes ● no | ● yes ○ no
2. ○ yes ● no | ○ yes ● no | ● yes ○ no
3. ● yes ○ no | ● yes ○ no | ○ yes ● no

TE Page 76 / SB Page 70

WEEK 24 DAY 1 Daily Math Practice

1. 7 + 4 = 11; 11 − 7 = 4
2. 14 − 8 = 6; 14 − 10 = 4
3. 34 > 31 ● yes ○ no; 27 > 72 ○ yes ● no
4. Color $\frac{1}{4}$ of all the balls.
5. One octopus and two divers are in the water. How many arms are there in all? 12 arms

WEEK 24 DAY 2 Daily Math Practice

1. 17 = 1 ten + 7 ones
2. 18 − 9 = 9
3. The truck holds ten crates, and the driver has loaded six. How many more crates does he need for a full load? 4 crates
4. How many? 17 tally marks
5.

ten more		ten less	
6	16	29	39
30	40	87	97

TE Page 77 / SB Page 71

WEEK 24 DAY 3 Daily Math Practice

1. 9 + 8 = 10 + 7 ● yes ○ no
2. 8 − 3 = 5; 5 + 3 = 8
3. Todd has three pencils, four markers, and twenty-two crayons. How many drawing tools does he have? 29 drawing tools
4. Circle the time. 1:00 (1:30) 6:00
5. If 23 + 5 = 28, then 28 − 5 = 23.

WEEK 24 DAY 4 Daily Math Practice

1. 7 + 7 = 14; 8 + 8 = 16
2. 18 − 5 = 13
3. Two frogs ate six flies. If each frog ate the same number of flies, how many did each frog eat? 3 flies
4. 69 < 50 ○ yes ● no; 47 < 74 ● yes ○ no
5. Continue the pattern. △○○□△○○□ △ ○ ○ △

TE Page 78 / SB Page 72

WEEK 24 DAY 5 Daily Math Practice

Each group of students planted ten seeds. Each seed can make one sprout. How many sprouting seeds did each group have?

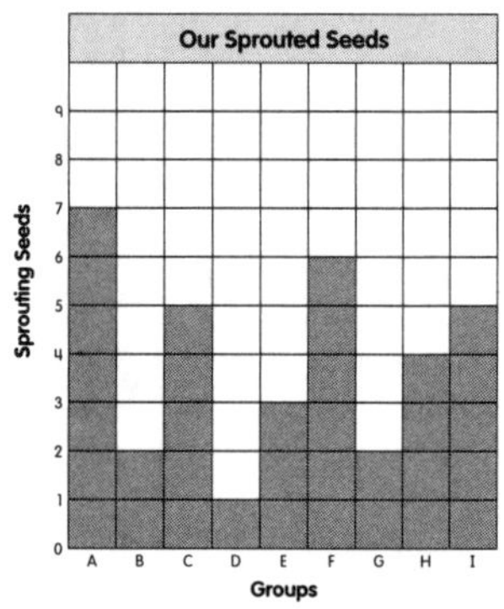

Group A 7 Group B 2 Group C 5
Group D 1 Group E 3 Group F 6
Group G 2 Group H 4 Group I 5

TE Page 79 / SB Page 73

WEEK 25 DAY 1 Daily Math Practice

1. 9 − 5 = 4 19 − 5 = 14

2. Luke has two boards. He needs four nails for each board. How many nails does he need?
 8 nails

3. 6 + 5 = 11 8 + 7 = 15 9 + 8 = 17

4. How much?

 35 cents

5. 65 64 63 62 61 60
 59 58 57 56 55

WEEK 25 DAY 2 Daily Math Practice

1. 2 + 4 − 2 + 1 = 5

2. Mark the pattern unit.
 △△□○△△□○
 ○ AAB ● AABC ○ ABC

3. If 5 + 23 = 28,
 then 23 + 5 = 28

4. Color the half circles.

5. There are six books on the table, three books on the chair, and ten books on the shelf. How many books are there in all?
 19 books

TE Page 80 / SB Page 74

WEEK 25 DAY 3 Daily Math Practice

1. 3 + 7 = 10

2. 8,247 + 0 = 8,247

3. Show four ways to make **12**.
 10 + 2 = 12
 6 + 6 = 12
 20 − 8 = 12
 14 − 2 = 12
 Answers will vary. Sample answers:

4. Draw an **X** on the line that is 2 paper clips long.

 A ______
 B ______ X
 C ______

5. **6** is an odd number.
 ○ yes ● no

WEEK 25 DAY 4 Daily Math Practice

1. 17 − 9 = 8

2. 7 + 6 + 4 = 17 7 + 10 = 17

3. Scott put six books, three pencils, and a notebook in his backpack. How many school supplies are in his backpack?
 10 school supplies

4. 100 + 10 + 9 = ?
 ○ 100 ● 119 ○ 19

5. How long is the gum?

 4 centimeters

TE Page 81 / SB Page 75

WEEK 25 DAY 5 Daily Math Practice

➤ **Activity 1**
What does **not** belong? Draw an **X** on it.

Tell how the other things are alike. Sample answers:
They are all things you can sit on.
OR They are all types of furniture.

➤ **Activity 2**
The dog ate my 100s chart!
Write the missing numbers.

47	48	49	50
57	58	59	60
67	68	69	70
77	78	79	80

TE Page 82 / SB Page 76

WEEK 26 DAY 1 Daily Math Practice

1. 9 + 10 = 19
 10 + 10 = 20

2. 16 − 8 = 8
 8 + 8 = 16

3. 20 25 30 35
 40 45 50

4. Circle the second star.

5. The ship has four red flags, seven green flags, and three yellow flags. How many flags does the ship have in all?
 14 flags

WEEK 26 DAY 2 Daily Math Practice

1. 8 + 5 = 13

2. 9 + 6 = 15

3. Write < or > to tell the rule:
 Group A: 1, 4, 3, 6, 2, 5
 All numbers are < 7.
 Group B: 8, 10, 9, 11, 13, 12
 All numbers are > 7.

4. Draw an **X** on the heaviest.

5. Each lunch bag has two sandwiches in it. How many sandwiches are in six bags?
 12 sandwiches

TE Page 83 / SB Page 77

WEEK 26 DAY 3 Daily Math Practice

1. 13 − 4 = 9
 13 − 3 = 10

2. If 41 + 8 = 49, then
 49 − 8 = 41.

3. The ladder has 18 rungs. Tom climbed halfway up. How many rungs did he climb?
 9 rungs

4. 2 + 20 = 22 4 + 20 = 24
 3 + 20 = 23 5 + 20 = 25

5. Color the circle green.
 Color the triangle black.
 Color the square pink.
 pink green black

WEEK 26 DAY 4 Daily Math Practice

1. 17 − 8 = 9
 8 + 9 = 17

2. 10 + 9 = 19

3. Mark the name for the shaded part.

 ○ $\frac{1}{4}$ ● $\frac{1}{3}$ ○ $\frac{1}{8}$

4. Five boys and seven girls sat in a row. Write a number sentence about the row.
 5 + 7 = 12

5. Circle the ways to make **9**.
 (8 + 1) 7 − 2 (3 + 6)
 (5 + 4) (9 − 0) (12 − 3)

TE Page 84 / SB Page 78

WEEK 26 DAY 5 Daily Math Practice

1. The soccer team scored four goals in their first game, five goals in their second game, and two goals in their third game. How many goals did they score in all?

 11 goals

Show your work here.

 4 first game
 5 second game
 + 2 third game
 11 goals in all

2. The team lost the third game. At least how many goals did the other team score?
 3 goals

Show your work here.

 2 goals scored
 + 1 goal winning team
 3 goals winning team

 The other team had to score at least 3 goals.

TE Page 85 / SB Page 79

WEEK 27 DAY 1 Daily Math Practice

1. 18 + 4 = 22
 22 − 18 = 4

2. 6 + 8 = 14
 14 − 6 = 8

3. Troy has 3 yellow cars, 7 green cars, and 6 white cars. How many cars does he have in all?
 16 cars

4. 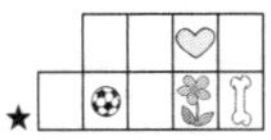
 Start at the star. Which answer tells how to find the ball?
 ○ left 2 boxes ● right 2 boxes

5. Write the number.
 fifteen 15 sixty 60
 fifty 50

WEEK 27 DAY 2 Daily Math Practice

1. 7 + 3 = 10
 17 + 3 = 20

2. 12 − 7 = 5
 7 + 5 = 12

3. Harry caught two ants, three crickets, and six beetles. How many bugs did he catch in all?
 11 bugs

4. 8 < 18 ● yes ○ no
 24 > 42 ○ yes ● no

5. About how many cans of apple juice?

 6 (12) 18

TE Page 86 / SB Page 80

WEEK 27 DAY 3 Daily Math Practice

1. 6 + 9 = 15
 9 + 6 = 15

2. 20 − 10 = 10
 30 − 10 = 20

3. Tim took four cookies. If he ate half of them, how many cookies did he eat?
 2 cookies

4. Write a story problem for **6 − 2 = ?**
 Sample answer:
 There were six fish.
 Two swam away. How
 many fish were left?

5. 5 + 4 = 6 + 3
 23 + 21 = 21 + 23
 Answers will vary. Sample answers:

WEEK 27 DAY 4 Daily Math Practice

1. 7 + 8 = 10 + 5
 ● yes ○ no

2. 17 − 8 = 9

3. Scott ate six pretzels, three cookies, and a brownie. How many snacks did he eat in all?
 10 snacks

4. Write four number sentences using **6**, **9**, and **15**.
 6 + 9 = 15
 9 + 6 = 15
 15 − 6 = 9
 15 − 9 = 6

5. Are both sides the same?

 ○ yes ● no

TE Page 87 / SB Page 81

WEEK 27 DAY 5 Daily Math Practice

➤ **Activity 1**
Match the pattern to its name.

➤ **Activity 2**
Show ways to make **15**. Use **+** and **−**.
Answers will vary. Sample answers:

7 + 8 = 15	20 − 5 = 15
8 + 7 = 15	19 − 4 = 15
10 + 5 = 15	18 − 3 = 15
5 + 10 = 15	17 − 2 = 15
14 + 1 = 15	16 − 1 = 15

TE Page 88 / SB Page 82

WEEK 28 DAY 1 Daily Math Practice

1. 13 − 5 = 8; 15 − 5 = 10
2. Count by 2s.
   20 22 24 26 28
   30 32 34 36
3. 12 + 2 = 14 The sum is an even number. ● yes ○ no
4. Write the number.
   ninety-one 91
   sixty-four 64
5. John ate $\frac{1}{2}$ of his sandwich for lunch and $\frac{1}{2}$ of his sandwich for a snack after school. How much is left?
   0 OR none is left

WEEK 28 DAY 2 Daily Math Practice

1. 6 + 3 + 2 = 11
2. 30 + 40 = 70
   35 + 40 = 75
3. What comes next?
   ○△△○△△○ △
4. How many?
   卌 卌 卌 卌 卌 卌 卌 ||
   37 tally marks
5. Juan had 105 marbles. His friend gave him 10 more. How many marbles does Juan have now?
   115 marbles

TE Page 89 / SB Page 83

WEEK 28 DAY 3 Daily Math Practice

1. 4 + 7 = 11
   11 − 7 = 4
2. 15 + 6 = 21
3. Circle the time.

   (5:00) 12:00 5:30
4. If 17 + 4 = 21, then 21 − 4 = 17
5. Mr. Brown asked 5 students to each bring 2 books they had read to the PTA meeting. How many books did they bring in all?
   10 books

WEEK 28 DAY 4 Daily Math Practice

1. 9 + 5 = 14
2. 15 + 0 = 15
3. Write a number sentence.
   6 − 2 = 4
   OR 3 + 3 = 6
4. Six cars were parked in the first row. Seven cars were parked in the second row. Five cars were parked in the third row. Which row had the most cars?
   ○ first ● second ○ third
5. 8 > 6 ● yes ○ no

TE Page 90 / SB Page 84

WEEK 28 DAY 5 Daily Math Practice

➤ **Activity 1**

Our Favorite Ice Cream Each scoop = 1 student

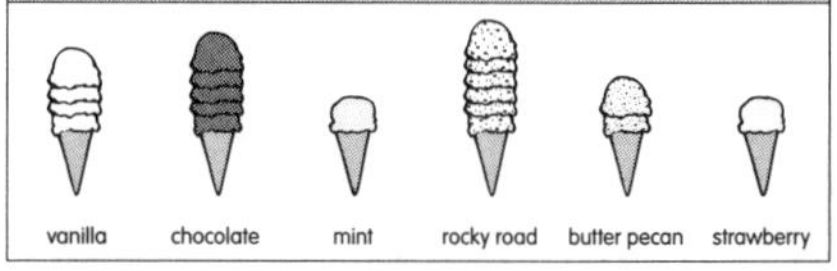

1. How many students like ice cream? 19 students
2. Which flavor do the students like best? rocky road
3. Do more students like butter pecan or vanilla? vanilla
4. Which flavor is your favorite? Answers will vary.

➤ **Activity 2**

Write the missing numbers.

	2		4		6		8	10
	12		14		16		18	20
	22		24		26		28	30
	32		34		36		38	40
	42		44		46		48	50

TE Page 91 / SB Page 85

WEEK 29 DAY 1 Daily Math Practice

1. 6 + 5 = 11
   5 + 6 = 11
2. 14 − 5 = 9
3. Sara's window has four corners and four equal sides. What shape is Sara's window?
   ○ triangle
   ● square
   ○ rectangle
4. How much?
   16 cents
5. Circle the even numbers.
   1 (2) 3 (4) 5 (6) 7 (8)

WEEK 29 DAY 2 Daily Math Practice

1. 8 + 7 = 15
2. 11 + 3 = 14; 12 + 2 = 14
3. Tessa has four brothers and two sisters. How many children are in Tessa's family?
   7 children
4. Which is longer?
   ○ one inch ● one foot
5. Write a story for **7 − 5 = ?**
   Sample answer:
   We had 7 cookies.
   We ate 5. How many
   cookies were left?

TE Page 92 / SB Page 86

WEEK 29 DAY 3 Daily Math Practice

1. 100 − 10 = 90
2. 16 = 1 ten + 6 ones
   40 = 4 tens + 0 ones
3. Carly sold three boxes of candy. Seth sold seven boxes. How many boxes did they sell altogether?
   10 boxes
4. Circle the shapes that have more than three sides.
5.

Add 10			
2	12	5	15
3	13	6	16
4	14	7	17

WEEK 29 DAY 4 Daily Math Practice

1. 19 + 10 = 29
2. 20 + 40 + 10 = 70
3. If Tina has ten puppies and four leashes, how many puppies do **not** have leashes?
   6 puppies
4. Write four number sentences using **10**, **11**, and **21**.
   10 + 11 = 21
   11 + 10 = 21
   21 − 10 = 11
   21 − 11 = 10
5. 8 + 9 = 17; 9 + 8 = 17

TE Page 93 / SB Page 87

WEEK 29 DAY 5 Daily Math Practice

➤ **Activity 1**

Each student needs two pencils and a ruler to do a project. If there are six students, how many pencils do they need altogether?

12 pencils

How many rulers do they need altogether?

6 rulers

Show your work.

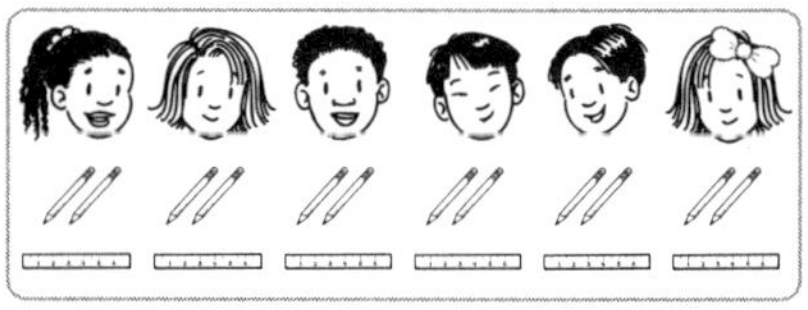

➤ **Activity 2**

2 + 2 + 2 + 2 + 2 + 2 = 12

5 + 5 + 5 + 5 = 20

10 + 10 + 10 + 10 + 10 = 50

TE Page 94 / SB Page 88

WEEK 30 DAY 1 Daily Math Practice

1. Draw an **X** on the sixth pin.
   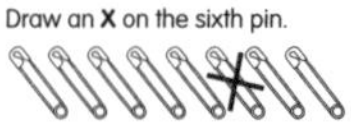
2. 4 + 8 = 12; 6 + 8 = 14; 8 + 8 = 16
3. How many letters are in Stephanie's name?
   9 letters
4. 25 30 35 40 45
   50 55 60 65
5. 5 + 5 = 10
   6 + 6 = 12
   7 + 7 = 14
   8 + 8 = 16
   9 + 9 = 18

WEEK 30 DAY 2 Daily Math Practice

1. 4 + 2 = 11
   10 + 2 = 12
2. 16 − 4 = 12
   4 + 12 = 16
3. Eight coconuts were on the tree. Three fell off. How many are left?
   5 coconuts
4. Write the time.
   12:00 12 o'clock
5. Color the beads. Make the spheres green. Make the cubes purple.
   P G P G

TE Page 95 / SB Page 89

WEEK 30 DAY 3 Daily Math Practice

1. 17 − 8 = 9
2. 5 + 5 + 5 = 15; 2 + 2 + 2 = 6
3. Minnie likes even numbers. Mickey likes odd numbers. Who likes **7**?
   ○ Minnie ● Mickey
4. Write an addition number sentence.

   1 + 5 + 10 = 16
5. Is 40 pounds heavier than 30 pounds?
   ● yes ○ no

WEEK 30 DAY 4 Daily Math Practice

1. 7 + 5 = 11 + 1 ● yes ○ no
2. 25 − 5 = 20
   5 + 20 = 25
3. There are four plates, four cups, and four forks on the table. How many people can eat?
   4 people
4. Show four ways to make **16**.
   8 + 8 = 16
   10 + 6 = 16
   20 − 4 = 16
   18 − 2 = 16
   Answers will vary. Sample answers:
5. If 8 + 9 = 17,
   then 17 = 9 + 8

TE Page 96 / SB Page 90

WEEK 30 DAY 5 Daily Math Practice

➤ **Activity 1**

I put six pretzels, four candies, and two cookies in my snack bag. How many things do I have in all?

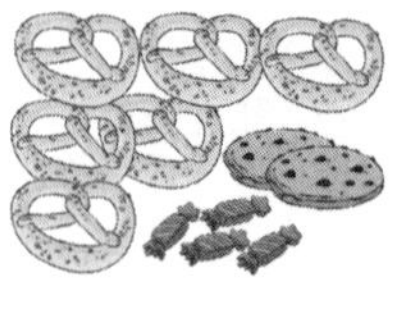

12 things

If I eat the pretzels, how many things will I have left?

6 things

Show your work.

6 pretzels
4 candies
+ 2 cookies
12 things in all

12 things
− 6 pretzels
6 things left

➤ **Activity 2**

Circle the left hand.
Draw an **X** on the right hand.

TE Page 97 / SB Page 91

WEEK 31 DAY 1 — Daily Math Practice

1. 6 + 4 = 7 + 3 ● yes ○ no
2. 5 + 6 = 11
   15 + 6 = 21
3. Tim had six paper clips. He used two on a puppet and two on a book. How many paper clips did he have left?
   2 paper clips
4. Color $\frac{1}{3}$ of all the pockets.

5. Match the words and numbers.

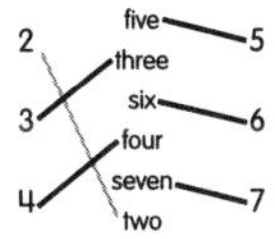

WEEK 31 DAY 2 — Daily Math Practice

1. 42 − 2 = 40; 67 − 5 = 62
2. 341 + 23 = 364; 404 + 32 = 436
3. Seven bees flew to four flowers. How many more bees than flowers were there?
   3 more bees
4. About how many toothpicks?

10 (100) 1,000

5. 9 < 9 ○ yes ● no
   9 > 9 ○ yes ● no
   9 = 9 ● yes ○ no

TE Page 98 / SB Page 92

WEEK 31 DAY 3 — Daily Math Practice

1. 16 − 8 = 8
2. Match each shape to its name.

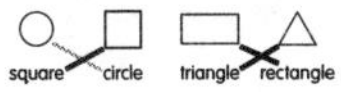

3. Liz put six black beads and six brown beads on her necklace. How many beads did she use in all?
   12 beads
4. Circle the ways to make **18**.
   (18 + 0)   17 + 2   (15 + 3)
5. Three girls played jump rope. Four boys played tag. Six other children played four square. How many children played in all?
   ○ 3 + 4 = 7
   ○ 3 + 4 + 6 = 17
   ● 3 + 4 + 6 = 13

WEEK 31 DAY 4 — Daily Math Practice

1. Continue the pattern.
   1 3 5 7 9 11 13
2. 4 + 7 + 2 = 13
3. Ava wants to fill a planter box. It holds five bags of soil. If Ava has two bags, how many more does she need?
   3 more bags
4. 15 − 5 = 10   25 − 5 = 20
   16 − 6 = 10   26 − 6 = 20
   17 − 7 = 10   27 − 7 = 20
5. Are the sides the same?

○ yes
● no

TE Page 99 / SB Page 93

WEEK 31 DAY 5 — Daily Math Practice

Activity 1

Show eight different ways to color the circles.
Use only red and blue. Plan before you color.

○R ○R ○R	○R ○B ○B	○R ○B ○R	○R ○B ○B
○B ○B ○B	○B ○B ○R	○B ○R ○B	○B ○R ○R

Activity 2

Rosa made a tower using four blocks as the base, three blocks for the next two levels, and one block on the top. How many blocks are in the tower?

11 blocks

Draw the tower.

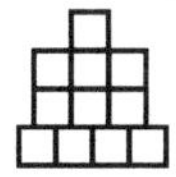

TE Page 100 / SB Page 94

WEEK 32 DAY 1 — Daily Math Practice

1. 67 − 52 = 15
2. 42 + 31 + 15 = 88; 23 + 51 + 22 = 96
3. Write the time.

half past 7

4. If 54 + 32 = 86,
   then 86 − 32 = 54
5. Drew needs a new pair of pants. He has \$10.00. If the pants cost \$8.00, how much change will he get?
   \$2.00

WEEK 32 DAY 2 — Daily Math Practice

1. 4 + 2 + 7 + 1 = 14
2. 5 + 3 − 2 = 6
3. Claire made a dozen cookies for her 6 friends. She will give the same number of cookies to each friend. How many will each friend get?
   2 cookies
4. Mark the name for the shaded part.

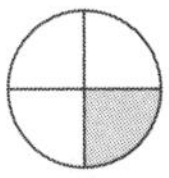

○ $\frac{1}{3}$
○ $\frac{2}{4}$
● $\frac{1}{4}$

5. Write the number.
   one hundred 100

TE Page 101 / SB Page 95

WEEK 32 DAY 3 — Daily Math Practice

1. 18 − 7 = 11
   7 + 11 = 18
2. 15 + 13 = 28
   28 − 15 = 13
3. 2 4 6 8 10 12
   2 + 2 + 2 + 2 + 2 + 2 = 12
4. 647 < 532 ○ yes ● no
   209 > 199 ● yes ○ no
5. Cindy has four nickels in her purse and two nickels in her pocket. How many nickels does she have in all?
   6 nickels
   How much are they worth?
   30¢

WEEK 32 DAY 4 — Daily Math Practice

1. 3 + 4 + 9 = 16
2. 9 − 2 − 3 = 4
3. Color the rectangles.

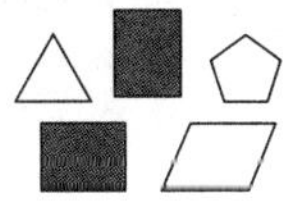

4. How many?

47 tally marks

5. Five frogs each ate five flies. How many flies did the frogs eat in all?
   25 flies

TE Page 102 / SB Page 96

WEEK 32 DAY 5 — Daily Math Practice

1. Count the letters in each name: **Lakesha**, **Teyo**, **Emily**, **Ayden**, **Jon**. Color the boxes on the graph to show the number of letters for each name.

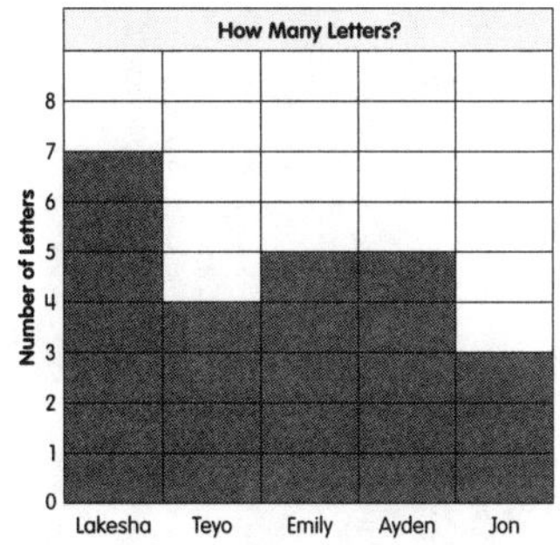

2. Write something you learned from the graph.
   Answers will vary. Sample answer:
   Emily's and Ayden's names have the same number of letters.

TE Page 103 / SB Page 97

WEEK 33 DAY 1 — Daily Math Practice

1. 5 + 8 = 13
   13 − 5 = 8
2. 14 − 9 = 5
   24 − 9 = 15
3. The fish tank has 6 guppies, 7 zebra fish, 1 catfish, and 1 snail. How many animals are in the fish tank?
   15 animals
4. How much?

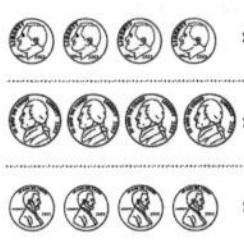

= 40 cents
= 20 cents
= 4 cents

5. 6 + 2 + 1 + 0 = 9

WEEK 33 DAY 2 — Daily Math Practice

1. 17 − 7 = 10
   17 − 8 = 9
   17 − 9 = 8
2. 14 + 6 = 20
3. 50 60 70 80 90
   100 110 120
4. Mark the pattern unit.
   ▲●▲♡▲●▲♡
   ● ABAC ○ ABAB ○ ABCA
5. The number is **73**.
   How many tens? 7
   How many ones? 3

TE Page 104 / SB Page 98

WEEK 33 DAY 3 — Daily Math Practice

1. 8 − 2 = 6; 18 − 2 = 16
2. 7 + 1 + 5 = 13; 8 + 5 = 13
3. Circle the ways to make **6**.
   (3 + 3)   (7 − 1)   2 + 5
   4 + 3   (5 + 1)   8 − 3
4. 84 = 8 tens + 4 ones
   70 = 7 tens + 0 ones
   55 = 5 tens + 5 ones
5. Dave found four eggs in a nest and five eggs in a basket. How many eggs did he find in all?
   9 eggs

WEEK 33 DAY 4 — Daily Math Practice

1. 8 + 9 = 17
   9 + 8 = 17
2. 18 − 6 = 12
   6 + 12 = 18
3. **32** is an odd number.
   ○ yes ● no
4. Color the figures with four corners and four sides.

5. Mia and Jo each picked four flowers. They put three in a vase. How many flowers are left?
   5 flowers

TE Page 105 / SB Page 99

WEEK 33 DAY 5 — Daily Math Practice

Activity 1

Jesse cut out three hearts, six circles, and three squares.
He made an **ABBC** repeating pattern using all the shapes.
Draw **two** patterns he could have made.

♡○○□♡○○□♡○○□

□○○♡□○○♡□○○♡

Activity 2

Draw an **ABCB** repeating pattern. Use triangles, rectangles, and circles.

△▯○▯△▯○▯

Answers will vary. Sample answer.

TE Page 106 / SB Page 100

WEEK 34 DAY 1 Daily Math Practice

1. 52 − 41 = 11; 74 − 23 = 51
2. 37 + 41 = 78; 85 + 12 = 97
3. Erik ate five pieces of pizza. If the pizza was cut into eight pieces, how many are left? 3 pieces
4. Draw an **X** on the tenth banana.

5. 10 + 2 = ? Circle the correct answers. (4 + 8) circled; 11 + 0; (9 + 3) circled

WEEK 34 DAY 2 Daily Math Practice

1. Two pounds > $\frac{1}{2}$ pound. ● yes ○ no
2. 73 + 14 + 12 = 99; 51 + 23 + 15 = 89
3. 5 10 15 20 25 30 35 40 45 50
4. Circle the clock that shows half past six. 6:00 12:30 (6:30) circled
5. Six kids each make two piles of sand. How many piles of sand are there in all? 12 piles

TE Page 107 / SB Page 101

WEEK 34 DAY 3 Daily Math Practice

1. 943 − 10 = 933
2. Circle the even numbers. 3 (8) 1 (6) (4) (2) 9
3. 7 + 10 = 17; 6 + 10 = 16; 7 + 100 = 107; 6 + 100 = 106
4. Twenty-six first graders are going to the dairy. A bus holds fourteen students. How many buses will they need? 2 buses

   How many extra seats will there be? 2 seats
5. seven (nickel)s = 35 cents

WEEK 34 DAY 4 Daily Math Practice

1. 8 + 2 + 5 + 3 = 18
2. If 25 + 34 = 59, then 59 − 34 = 25
3. 9 − 9 = 0; 8 − 8 = 0; 7 − 7 = 0; 6 − 6 = 0
4. Ronni rode her bike 8 blocks to Joe's house and back home. How many blocks did Ronni ride by the time she got home? 16 blocks
5. Write a number sentence to show how many legs there are.

6 + 6 + 6 + 6 = 24

TE Page 108 / SB Page 102

WEEK 34 DAY 5 Daily Math Practice

1. Look at the data. Color one square on the graph for each book.

Data	
animal books	𝍸 III
fairy tales	𝍸 II
sports books	II
chapter books	IIII
holiday books	𝍸

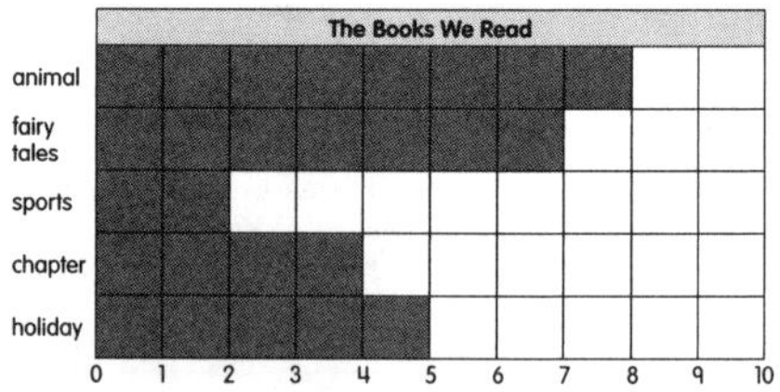

2. Look at the graph and write something you learned. Answers will vary. Sample answer: More children read animal books than any of the other types.

TE Page 109 / SB Page 103

WEEK 35 DAY 1 Daily Math Practice

1. 4 + 5 + 3 + 0 = 12
2. Are the two parts the same? ○ yes ● no
3. If Daren pops three balloons, how many balloons will be left? 6 balloons
4. 11 + 10 = 21; 12 + 10 = 22; 13 + 10 = 23; 14 + 10 = 24; 15 + 10 = 25
5. 10 20 30 40 50 60 70 80 90 100 110 120 130

WEEK 35 DAY 2 Daily Math Practice

1. 17 − 8 = 9
2. 8 + 1 + 4 = 13
3. At the movies, 4 children are in the fourth row, 3 in the third row, 2 in the second row, and 1 in the first row. How many children are there in all? 10 children
4. If 64 − 33 = 31, then 64 − 31 = 33
5. Write an addition number sentence. 8 + 8 = 16

TE Page 110 / SB Page 104

WEEK 35 DAY 3 Daily Math Practice

1. 5 + 2 + 7 = 14
2. 8 − 4 = 4; 38 − 34 = 4
3. At the game, Alec made 4 goals. He scored two points for each goal. How many points did he score in all? 8 points
4. Continue the pattern. ○ ○ □ ○ ○ □ ○ ○ □
5. About how many marshmallows? (more than 20) circled; less than 20

WEEK 35 DAY 4 Daily Math Practice

1. 62 + 37 = 99; 37 + 62 = 99
2. 19 − 8 = 11; 19 − 9 = 10
3. How many sides? one square = 4 sides; two squares = 8 sides
4. 90 80 70 60 50 40 30 20 10 0
5. Michael is 48 inches tall. Sandi is 2 inches taller than Michael. How many inches tall is Sandi? 50 inches

TE Page 111 / SB Page 105

WEEK 35 DAY 5 Daily Math Practice

Activity 1

Look at the grid. Show how to find each animal. Begin at the star.

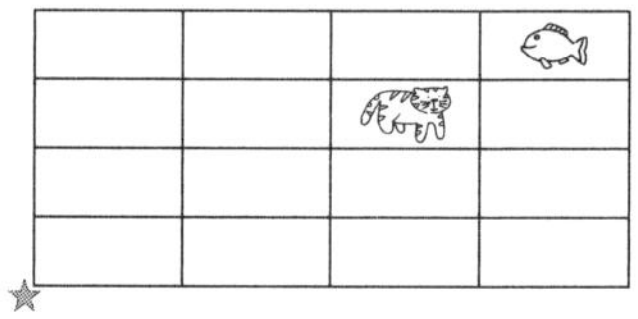

1. (fish) over 4, up 4
2. (cow) over 3, up 3

Activity 2

Color the numbers to count by fives.

1	2	3	4	5	6	7	8	9	10
11	12	13	14	15	16	17	18	19	20
21	22	23	24	25	26	27	28	29	30
31	32	33	34	35	36	37	38	39	40
41	42	43	44	45	46	47	48	49	50
51	52	53	54	55	56	57	58	59	60
61	62	63	64	65	66	67	68	69	70
71	72	73	74	75	76	77	78	79	80
81	82	83	84	85	86	87	88	89	90
91	92	93	94	95	96	97	98	99	100

TE Page 112 / SB Page 106

WEEK 36 DAY 1 Daily Math Practice

1. 325 − 214 = 111
2. Color $\frac{1}{4}$.
3. Sabir has two trucks, seven cars, and an ambulance. How many vehicles does he have in all? 10 vehicles
4. Write the correct symbol in the circle. < = > 38 < 46; 68 < 79
5. Circle the time. 4:00 (4:30) circled 6:00

WEEK 36 DAY 2 Daily Math Practice

1. 47 + 22 = 69
2. 5 + 10 + 4 + 10 = 29; 15 + 14 = 29
3. Continue the pattern. 21 + 0 22 + 0 23 + 0 24 + 0 25 + 0
4. How many? 𝍸 𝍸 𝍸 𝍸 𝍸 𝍸 III — 33 tally marks
5. There are twenty parking spaces in the lot. Fifteen cars are parked. How many spaces are empty? 5 spaces

TE Page 113 / SB Page 107

WEEK 36 DAY 3 Daily Math Practice

1. 89 − 34 = 55
2. 73 + 15 = 88
3. Seven friends went to the store. They each had two dollars to spend. How much money did they have altogether? $14.00
4. Count by 2s. 72 74 76 78 80 82 84 86 88 90
5. Write the number. forty-one 41; forty-four 44; forty-nine 49; fifty-two 52

WEEK 36 DAY 4 Daily Math Practice

1. 24 + 43 = 67
2. 38 − 6 = 32
3. Joy has seven eggs. How many more eggs does she need to fill the carton? 5 eggs
4. Continue the pattern. △ ▽ △ ▽ △ ▽ △ ▽
5. Circle the clock that shows the same time. (6:00) circled; 12:00; 12:30

TE Page 114 / SB Page 108

WEEK 36 DAY 5 Daily Math Practice

1. Josh wanted to sort his Legos®. Think about how he could sort them into two groups.

2. Draw to show which shapes would go in each group. Then write the rule. Answers will vary. Sample answer:

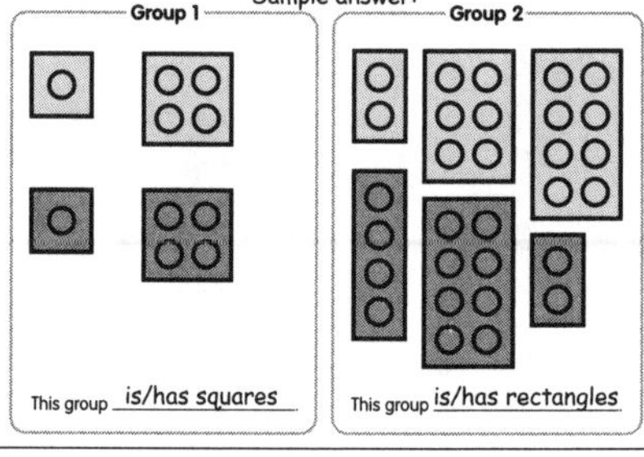

Group 1 — This group is/has squares

Group 2 — This group is/has rectangles

Math Fundamentals

Grades 1–6

Demystify the new math with ***Math Fundamentals***!

Math Fundamentals is a comprehensive resource that can be used to review math skills, provide additional practice, and remediate and target instruction for struggling students.

The math models and problem-solving templates in this book will guide your students through successfully analyzing and solving grade-level math problems. And the math models are also helpful for parents!

Mathematical practices and standards are included for each unit for easy reference.

Math Fundamentals can also be used for core math practice correlated to the most current standards.

Correlated to current standards.

Teacher's Edition*

Grade 1	EMC 3081
Grade 2	EMC 3082
Grade 3	EMC 3083
Grade 4	EMC 3084
Grade 5	EMC 3085
Grade 6	EMC 3086

**Available in print and e-book*

Better Together

Complements the skill practice in:
Daily Math Practice

Financial Literacy Grades 1–8

Lessons & Activities

Help students apply math to the world around them!

Give students important life skills by teaching them about money and how to apply math to the world around them. The real-life examples and authentic games and activities in this dynamic series engage students in applying financial concepts to life, while also applying higher-order thinking skills across the curriculum.

- Real-world stories
- Math applications
- Interesting topics

Books include reproducible resource pages with cutouts, reference sheets, and additional aids to support student learning.

144 reproducible pages.

Teacher Resource Book*

Grade 1	EMC 3121
Grade 2	EMC 3122
Grade 3	EMC 3123
Grade 4	EMC 3124
Grade 5	EMC 3125
Grades 6–8	EMC 3126

**Available in print and e-book*

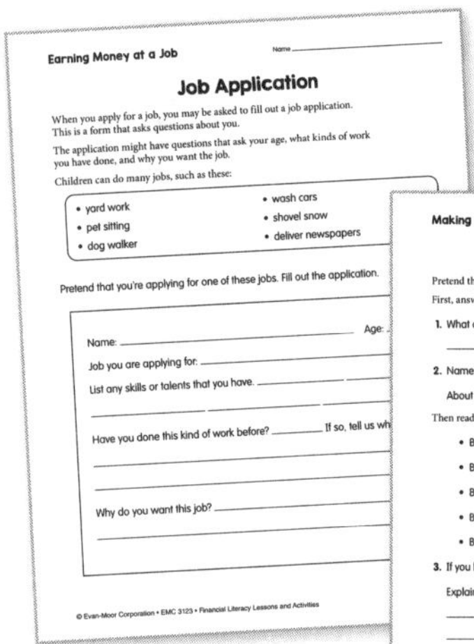

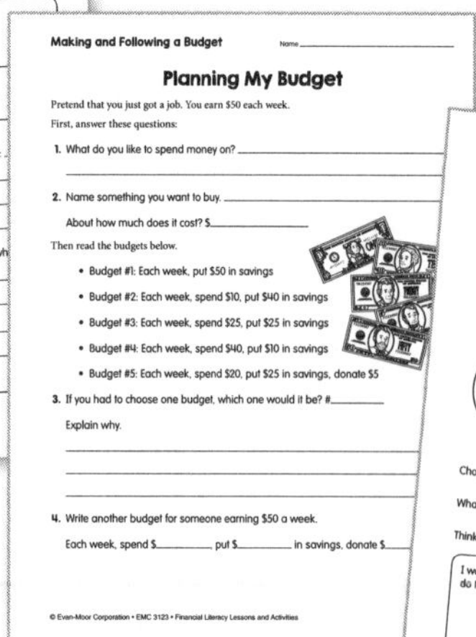

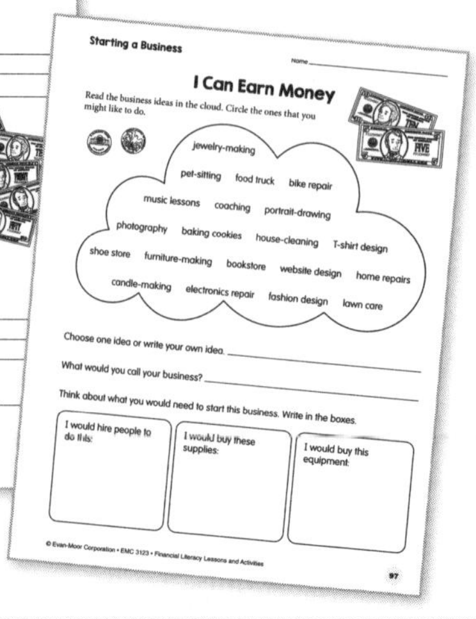

Grade 3